P9-EER-804

DATE DUE

THE NEW SOUND/YES!

Edited by Ira Peck

INTRODUCTION
BY MURRAY THE K

THE FOUR WINDS PRESS • NEW YORK

For reprint and abridgment permission grateful acknowledgment is made to:

Peter Bart for "The California Sound" by Peter Bart. Copyright © 1965 by The Atlantic Monthly Company.

Ebony Magazine for "Rock 'n' Roll Becomes Respectable" by Louie Robinson. Copyright © 1965 by *Ebony*.

Farrar, Straus & Giroux, Inc. for "The First Tycoon of Teen" from THE KANDY KOLORED TANGERINE FLAKE STREAMLINE BABY by Tom Wolfe. Copyright © 1965 by New York Herald Tribune, Inc.

The Sterling Lord Agency for "Music's Gold Bugs: The Beatles" by Alfred G. Aronowitz from the *Saturday Evening Post*. Copyright © 1964 by Alfred G. Aronowitz.

William Morris Agency, Inc. for "One Near-Square Who Doesn't Knock the Rock" by James Michener from *The New York Times*. Copyright © 1965 by Marjay Productions, Inc.

Russell & Volkening, Inc. for "What Do They Get From Rock 'n' Roll?" by Jeremy Larner from *The Atlantic Monthly*. Copyright © 1964 by The Atlantic Monthly Company; for "The New Sounds of Rock 'n' Roll Music'" by Bruce Jay Friedman from *Holiday*. Copyright © 1965 by Curtis Publishing Company, Inc.

Time The Weekly Newsmagazine for "The Sound of the Sixties." Copyright © 1965 by Time Inc.

Vernon Scott for "Elvis—Ten Million Dollars Later" by Vernon Scott from *McCall's*. Copyright © 1963 by McCall Corporation.

Henrietta Yurchenco for "In Defense of Bob Dylan" from *Sounds and Fury*. Copyright © 1966 by Castell Publishing Co.

Published by The Four Winds Press, a division of Scholastic Magazines, Inc., New York, N.Y.

THE NEW SOUND/YES!

YEAH YEAH YEAH   YEAH YEAH YEAH   YEAH YEAH YEAH   YEAH YEAH YEAH

CONTENTS

3. WHY?

ABOUT THE NEW SOUND
Murray the K

When I heard that Scholastic was preparing a book about pop music for young readers, I was delighted, and I jumped at the chance to write a preface for it.

Music seems a pleasant, inoffensive subject that interests all Americans. But music can become a very controversial subject when discussed or written about, except when the writer sticks strictly to facts. Because of its very personal appeal, it can become as controversial a subject as religion or politics.

Music discussions usually bring out quite unexpected prejudices and attitudes in people. The way in which someone discusses music and what he says about it can tell you a great deal about him.

Music's main purpose is to entertain. Sometimes it communicates ideas or stimulates new thoughts and emotions, sad or glad.

There are all kinds of music fans. The fellows relate to music in one manner and can get "hung up" on a certain sound, while girls are apt to get "hung up," not only on a song, but on the performers as well. That's why girls spend so much more money for records than do boys. They have an emotional involvement. Among pop-music devotees there are several cliques. I have written about one such clique in my new book called *Murray the K Tells It Like It Is, Baby* (published by Holt, Rinehart and Winston), in which I have a subchapter entitled "The Folk Purists," or "How to Become a Bigot Without Knowing It."

You'll notice that I refer to today's music as "pop music," preferring to stay away from the term "rock 'n' roll," which I believe is no longer applicable. We now have a potpourri of pop sounds which you will find described throughout this book. I believe that rock 'n' roll belonged to the Bill Haley era. Today so many types of music can become "hits" — jazz, folk rock, or what I call "attitude music," the California sound, rhythm and blues, country music, a hit from a musical comedy, novelty, instrumental, etc. — that it is impossible to put the limitation of a rock-'n'-roll label on most current music. It can only be labeled in broad terms like "today's music," "pop music," or "the new sound."

The music created today *is* new and exciting. The music itself is far ahead of its manner of presentation on both radio and TV. New lyrical attitudes and new musical sounds have been found by today's writers and record producers. It is now up to radio disc jockeys and TV music shows to advance *their* presentation of this new musical expression. In other words, radio and TV must find a new frame of reference for today's music explosion.

The days of Thornton Wilder and Irving Berlin are over, and — hard as it is for the parents of today's students to realize this — life no longer exists as Wilder and Berlin painted it. Today's songs reflect attitudes of children born after the close of World War II, whose psyche was fathered by the atom bomb!

This new sound is expressing some very important contemporary attitudes, and what its lyrics cry for most is *honesty* and today's values. I believe adults and educators have the responsibility to learn about and understand these new attitudes before they can qualify to deal with the subject of today's music. Most students are ahead of their elders in relating to what the new sound expresses about their own attitudes and the age we live in.

Rock 'n' Roll: The Sound of the Sixties

Time Magazine

What is rock 'n' roll? Where did it come from? What are its most significant milestones? Why is it more popular today than ever before? The following history of rock 'n' roll answers these and other questions.

The Trashmen. The Kinks. Goldie and the Gingerbreads. The Ripchords. Bent Fabric. Reparata and the Delrons. Barry and the Remains. The Pretty Things. The Emotions. The Detergents. Sam the Sham and the Pharaohs. The Guess Who's. Cannibal and the Headhunters. Them. The Orlons. The Liverbirds. Wump and the Werbles. Like something out of *Malice in Wonderland*, the hordes of shaggy rock-'n'-roll singers thump across the land, whanging their electric guitars. Bizarre as they may be, they are the anointed purveyors of the big beat and, as never before, people are listening — all kinds of people.

For the past ten years social commentators, with more hope than insight, have been predicting that rock would roll over and die the day after tomorrow. Yet it is still very much here — front, center, and belting out from extra speakers on the unguarded flank. Many

cannot take rock 'n' roll, but no one can leave it. The
big beat is everywhere. It resounds over TV and radio,
in saloons and soda shops, fraternity houses and dance
halls. It has become, in fact, the international anthem
of a new and restless generation, the pulse beat for
new modes of dress, dance, language, art, and moral-
ity. The sledge-hammer refrains of Wayne Fontana
and the Mind Benders' "Um, Um, Um, Um, Um, Um"
can be heard parting the walls of a Yokohama teahouse,
a recreation room in Topeka, or a Communist youth
club in Warsaw. For better or worse, like it or loathe
it, rock 'n' roll is the sound of the sixties.

The origins of rock 'n' roll go deep — Deep South,
U.S.A. There, in the 1930's, in the fields and shanties
of the delta country, evolved an earthy, hard-driving
style of music called "rhythm and blues" — played by
Negroes for Negroes. Cured in misery, it was a lone-
some, soul-sad music, full of cries and gospel wails,
punctuated by a heavy, regular beat. With the migra-
tion to the industrial North after World War II, the
beat was intensified with electric guitars, bass and
drums, and the great blues merchants, like Muddy
Waters, Bo Diddley, John Lee Hooker, and Chuck
Berry, made their first recordings.

One of the first white disc jockeys to play these
"race records," as they were known in the industry,
was Cleveland's Alan Freed, a flamboyant, rapid-fire
pitchman who sang along with the records, slamming
his hand down on a telephone book to accentuate each
beat. Borrowing a phrase used in several rhythm-and-
blues songs, Freed christened the music "rock 'n' roll."
Gradually, the big beat began to take hold.

Then, in the fall of 1956, came Elvis Presley with

his flapping hair, three-inch sideburns, and gyrating hips. "Ah wa-ha-hunt yew-hoo, Ah nee-hee-heed yew-hoo," he sang, and millions of teen-agers flipped.

There was obviously something visceral about Elvis and his music. Because soon there were riots in Hartford, Atlanta, and San Jose, California. Theaters were demolished in London and São Paulo, Brazil. Sociologists began to view the phenomenon with alarm. Studies showing that Elvis fans had a below-C average were circulated. A Senate subcommittee started to investigate the link between the rock 'n' roll and juvenile delinquency. Pablo Casals condemned rock 'n' roll as "poison put to sound," Frank Sinatra called it a "rancid-smelling aphrodisiac," and Samuel Cardinal Stritch labeled it "tribal rhythms."

Then, in 1959, the Payola scandal struck. Freed was indicted for accepting $30,000 in bribes from six record companies for pushing their releases. Rock 'n' roll faltered; record sales fell off 30 per cent. Crooned Bing Crosby, "My kind of music is coming back."

But it didn't. Instead, rock 'n' roll did. Rejuvenation came in 1960 on the wings of a king-sized twister named Chubby Checker. A onetime Philadelphia chicken plucker, Chubby threw his tubby hips into high gear and issued an invitation, "C'mon, baby, let's do the Twist!"

The Twist did not seem like much of an invention at the time. The participant merely planted his feet opposite his partner, started churning his arms as if shadowboxing, while rotating his hips like a girl trying to wriggle out of a tight girdle. But it transformed rock 'n' roll from a noise on the transistor radio into a teen-age style. For the first time since the decline of the Jitterbug, teen-agers had a new dance, and soon, at Manhattan's Peppermint Lounge, the famous and near-famous discovered its uninhibited joys.

Even then, rock 'n' roll was still dismissable among the sophisticates as a curiously persistent fad. But then came the British. American parents had weathered Pat Boone's white-bucks period, the histrionics of Johnnie Ray, and the off-key mewings of Fabian, but this was something else again — four outrageous Beatles in high-heeled boots, undersized suits, and enough hair between them to stuff a sofa. When they appeared on the "Ed Sullivan Show" in February, 1964, 68,000,000 people, one of the largest TV audiences in history, tuned in to see what all the ruckus was about.

What they saw was four young chaps having a jolly good bash. In the avalanche of publicity that followed, the Beatles emerged as refreshingly relaxed, if not downright lovable, personalities. Their disarming humor (Reporter: "Why do you wear so many rings on your fingers?" Ringo: "Because I can't get them all through my nose") melted adult resistance. By refusing to take themselves seriously, the Beatles made rock 'n' roll fun again.

The Beatles also made it all right to be white. As French critic Frank Tenot notes, "Since the downfall of the Viennese waltz, nothing in popular music, and particularly dance, has known any success unless associated with one or another of the rhythmic discoveries of the Negro." Beatle music (known as the "Mersey sound") and even Beatle accents are actually Anglicized imitations of Negro rhythm and blues once

Chuck Berry

removed. Says Beatle John Lennon, "We can sing more colored than the Africans."

Among the many white rock-'n'-roll singers attempting a pure "brown sound" today, the most successful are the Righteous Brothers and the Rolling Stones. The Righteous Brothers, a Mutt-and-Jeff pair of twenty-four-year-old Californians, are referred to by Negro disc jockeys as "our blue-eyed soul brothers."

To distinguish themselves from the Beatles, Britain's Rolling Stones have attempted to assume the image of Angry Young Men. "The Stones," their manager proudly explains, "are the troupe that parents love to hate." They sing Mersey-Mississippi rhythm and blues, backed by a quavering guitar and a chugging harmonica that smacks of cotton-pickin' time down South.

The best brown sound is, of course, that sung by Negroes. In 1964, forty-two of the best-selling rock-'n'-roll songs were produced by one man: Berry Gordy, Jr., thirty-five, who as head of Detroit's Motown Records, employs some 175 Negro artists. Next to the Mersey sound, the "Motown sound" currently dominates the rock-'n'-roll market. It is a swingy city-blues sound, propelled by a driving beat, tambourines, violins (from the Detroit Symphony), hand clapping, and an ever-present "Oh yeah, oh yeah" refrain from the chorus.

The prize fillies in Gordy's stable are the Supremes, three girls who grew up together in Detroit's squalid Brewster Housing Project. With four consecutive Number 1 records, they are the reigning female rock-'n'-roll group, followed by Motown's Martha and the Vandellas. Diana Ross, twenty-one, the Supreme's lead singer, is greatly envied for the torchy, come-hither purr in her voice.

Distinct from the brown-sound school are the Beach Boys from California. "We're not colored; we're white. And we sing white." They made their big splash with the "surf sound" — clean, breezy orchestration, a jerky, staccato beat, and a high, falsetto quaver reminiscent of the Four Freshmen. The Beach Boys' tenor harmony goes so high that it sounds almost feminine, a fact that has all but locked out girl singers from the scores of surf groups performing on the West Coast. They write their own songs, following one rule of thumb: "We picture the United States as one great big California."

Last year the man of the moment was Herman, sixteen, of Herman's Hermits. An engaging high-school dropout who looks like a toy sheep dog, Herman (real name Peter Noone) smiles a lot, claps his hands over his head, and sticks his finger in his mouth when he sings. His "Mrs. Brown, You've Got a Lovely Daughter," rendered in a heavy English Midlands accent, was the Number 1 best seller.

Rock-'n'-roll lyrics have lately taken on urban socio-economic themes. In the Crystals' "Uptown," downtown is a place where a man "don't get no breaks" and "everyone's his boss, and he's lost in an angry land." But to hear Petula Clark on the subject, "Downtown" is an island of promise.

Rock 'n' roll still does not exactly have the *Good Housekeeping* seal of approval. But even the most recalcitrant of parents now say, "Well, some of it's O.K." Some of it, in fact, is very good — far better than the adenoidal lamentations of a few years ago.

Some of it is still awful, as might be expected in an
industry that grinds out more than 300 new records
each week. But for the first time rock 'n' roll can boast
a host of singers who can actually sing. The music,
once limited to four chords, is now more sophisticated,
replete with counterrhythms, advanced harmonics, and
multivoiced choirs. Rock recordings, says jazz critic
Ralph Gleason, "are a lot more interesting than the
average jazz release." Conductor Leonard Bernstein
likes the Beatles and does not hesitate to admit it:
"They are very intelligent, and they have made songs
which are really worthwhile. 'Love Me Do' is really
stirring and very reminiscent in some ways of Hindu
music."

Above all, rock 'n' roll today is lively, youthful,
aggressive, often funny, seldom heartsick. The lyrics,
showing the influence of folk music, are fresher and
more intelligible. Coming the other way, the folk types
are beginning to feel the beat. Drums and electric
guitars, long scorned by folkniks as decadent com-
mercialism, are now featured on the latest album by
Bob Dylan, folkdom's crown prince.

Meanwhile, as expressed in the folk-rock song
"Walk Right In," the invitation to join in the big beat
is there for the accepting — with a slight qualifier:

> Walk right in, sit right down.
> Baby, let your hair hang down.
> Everybody's talkin' 'bout a new way of walkin'.
> Do you want to lose your mind?

THE NEW SOUNDS

Bruce Jay Friedman

If a rock-'n'-roll group wants to last longer than four and a half minutes, it'd better have a distinctive new sound, because the kids are fickle, always looking for something new, new, new. What about the music they make? Some of it is plain, all-out bad; and some of it is tender and powerful, obviously rooted in the classics. If you give it a chance, the best of the music will steal into your blood, whether you're U Thant or Ladybird Johnson.

It has been called bad, dirty, offensive, loud, obscene, and it may be that much of this labeling is deserved. Yet it seems to me that much of rock-'n'-roll music is also sweet and innocent, tender and vital, and that a visit to this world is a chance to roll back the membrane of youth's dreams. You peer inside and then you put one foot in, and before you know it you are strolling around and have decided to buy some property so that you can always return. You may notice that, in a curious way, you have always lived there.

The first visit is a dizzying, zigzag ride through a Coney Island jungle. The music and lyrics flail out at

you, choked with alien sounds, some of them expect-
edly raucous, hyenalike; others gentle, soft as tongues.
There is advice you don't need, suffocating clichés,
but then flashes of skin-pinching wisdom, sounds and
talk so current they make your teeth chatter.

It is a tangled world, where often simplistic, brain-
dulling lyrics are blended with spiraling, vine-entan-
gled, suddenly thrilling, cathedral-like backgrounds.
Boys sound like girls, girls like boys, authentic Negro
rhythm and blues singers turn out to be deep-banged
David Copperfield types from the slums of Liverpool.
Children slip into manhood almost in mid-record, and
for a while the whole world seems to be named Bobby.
A thigh-slapping country boy makes himself heard;
a crowd of harmonizing nuns, chanting hipster rabbis,
strange, sexless creatures from Australia, surfers from
Los Angeles. Latins swing into view ("Hey, Baby, You
Want to Dance with Me?"), trailing groups of spindly,
gospel-cloaked Negro girls who sing with a new pride
snatched from civil-rights marches. Suddenly, without
explanation, as though let in on visas, there are Dean
Martin, Tony Bennett, Robert Goulet. With amused
wisdom, looking down from on high: Presley in his
thirties.

There are the voices of winners ("I'm in Love with
Her and I Feel Fine") and, more often, the sound of
losers ("Mr. Lonely"). Riding through so much of it
is the sound of youth — jukebox tinkling, defiant brat-
tiness, skirts swishing, grown-up putdowns, kisses refused, engines grunting, swirling figures, guitars, lone-
liness, backs suddenly turned, movie-house wrestling,
and death on the highway.

Popping up bravely, then disappearing like wild

flowers in the path of a lawnmower, are the endless
groups: the Ronettes, the You-Know-Whos, the Rolling Stones, the Miracles, the Delrons, Searchers, Supremes, Honeycombs, Temptations, Exciters, Shangri-
Las, Orlons, Impressions, Devotions. One expects the
list to continue endlessly.

There is a musical explanation for it: the big bands
became outmoded, uneconomical. A small group of
kids could do the same job, cost less. But you feel
there is more. It is as though the kids are huddling
together, fearful of standing alone, afraid to hear the
sounds of their single voices.

Some of the groups are chaotic, cannibal-like, un-
ruly gangs, just moving and shouting, really, as if to
drown out the massive Jack Ruby chord of absurdity
that has been struck in the land. If they move enough,
moan enough, cry and entreat enough, it will all go
away. Others do a numb, glazed-eyed, much-sought-
after "dumb sound." You know about this one if you
have ever gone all the way down the line in argument
with an adolescent, watched him retreat behind a final,
immovable, no-grownups-allowed barrier. The dumb
sound exists behind this last sullen barricade.

And then there are the groups that send out a sound
tying rock 'n' roll of all shades together — an insis-
tent, deep-probing, suffocating beat that laces through
your middle to pull at stale, long-unplucked chords of
youth. The music is innocently in the style of a young,
pretty girl who crosses and rocks her legs while knit-
ting argyles. If you give it a chance, the best of the
music (the Supremes, Beatles, Dion Warwick, Maxine
Brown, Lesley Gore, the Impressions) will steal into
your blood, and whether you are U Thant or Ladybird

Johnson, don't bet that your feet won't begin to move.

It cannot, of course, be explained, any more than you can explain why a boy is in love with monster movies one day, leopard frogs the next, girls the day after that. Trying to sort out rock-'n'-roll tastes is like making sense out of the contents of an enormous shoulder bag belonging to every American teen-age cheerleader.

You pay attention to the "Top Fifty" if you are in the rock-'n'-roll industry — a list as scrambled and disarrayed as the mind of a schizophrenic. One week, a sweet easy-rocking Beatles ballad ("I Want to Hold Your Hand") stands back to back with "The Battle Hymn of the Republic," by the Salt Lake City Tabernacle Choir. A wild-eyed rock-'n'-roll standard by Dobie Gray ("I'm In with the In Crowd." — *We get respect from the people we meet . . . Our share is always the biggest amount*) locks arms with the warming and religion-steeped "O'Bambino" of the Harry Simeone Chorale. "Ringo," a western ballad by Lorne Greene, a man of television, stranger to rock 'n' roll, crowds an Al Hirt jazz instrumental. The next week you expect the Beatles to dominate the list, but suddenly they are nowhere in sight, their place taken by the swarming, junglelike Righteous Brothers, a child named Little Anthony who thinks he's going out of his head, the Searchers describing the wonders of love potion Number 9 ("I Didn't Know if It Was Day or Night, I Started Kissin' Everything in Sight").

It is no business for the parasites and imitators. Tastes change so swiftly that if you try to repeat the

The Animals

success of the Shangri-Las, the Kinks, Alvin Cash and
the Crawlers, you find to your dismay that there are
no longer any Shangri-Las, Kinks, and Crawlers to
imitate. I was sick for several weeks, during which I
stopped listening to the music (you seem to need your
health for rock-'n'-roll listening). When I returned,
it was as though I had gotten off a train at the wrong
stop and was walking in a new neighborhood. Winner
songs were out, loser tunes were in. The Animals were
gone, the Zombies had taken command. Where were
Joe Hinton, Martha and the Vandellas? Elbowed aside
by Petula Clark, Dick and Deedee.

The music may be untamed, chaotic, but it is this
very quality that has rendered the rock-'n'-roll radio
station managers, the people who decide what to play
and not to play, modest and humble. No man among
them feels confident that he can pick hits, can say for
sure what the kids will like or reject. They are not
only modest but awestruck, flabbergasted by the many
tails of this rock-'n'-roll dragon. A record-company
man talking: "The standard procedure is for a group
of these kids to make a hit, sell a million records, and
then, two months later, be right back in the butcher
shop in Topeka wondering what ever happened to
them."

"Sound" is the word that reels triumphantly through
all echelons of the rock-'n-'roll industry; you'd better
have a distinctive one if you are going to be around
longer than four and a half minutes. A deejay invites
his audience to listen not to a record but to a sound,
the way a fashion house shows off a look. The records
that succeed wear their sounds like identifying badges;
you can tell them miles away, in the dark or with one

ear tied behind your back. Lesley Gore — spunky, ripe-apple fresh, no nonsense, and if you're a boy she'll knock sense into your head ("I Don't Wanna Be a Loser"); the Zombies — tense, thin-chested, scared of girls ("If She Tempts You with Her Charms, Tell Her No, No, No, Nonononononono"); the Righteous Brothers — unshaven, dressed up for the first time, like Mafia men suddenly thrust into Sicilian choirs; Dobie Gray — pimpled, falsely cocky, scared out of his wits though in with the In crowd; the Beachboys lonely, rudderless, mooning, riding twenty-foot waves to an uncertain future.

Very often the sound that sticks is the one that makes you gnash your teeth, turn the dial the first time you hear it — Joe Tex giving you the worst advice in the world ("Girls, This Goes for You." — *If you think nobody wants your man, just pitch him out the door and you will see . . . someone else will have him before you can count one, two, three*); Joe Hinton, his whining lament ("Someday You're Gonna Pay") making you cringe with shame for the entire male sex. And just as the book publisher has little patience with the novelist who writes "just like Bellow" or is "another Updike," the rock-'n'-roll world quickly buries the group "you can't tell from the Four Seasons" or the singer who's "a dead-ringer for Diane Renay." In his stick-with-me-baby world of wide ties and greased pompadours, Joe Petralia, a top record-promotion man, knows one thing: "I don't care if he picks his teeth or pounds a washboard, a kid has got to have a sound to stay alive. With Chad and Jeremy, it's a smooth, pretty thing. Checker, of course, has got the unique twist sound. We've already had forty-two

Johnny Mathis sounds, all of them dead as a herring —
Johnny Nash, Billy Storm, Adam Wade. What did
we need them for when we had Mathis? A new sound,
always something new, new, new. The kids are Mr.
Fickle. Presley used to breathe and it was a hit. Not
any more. It's got to be new, different, unique." The
sound may show up anywhere — a high-school gym,
kids fooling around in front of a drugstore.

The search for new sounds goes on with the same
assiduity the Pentagon uses in rooting out new weap-
ons. Sound is the passport, the currency of acceptance,
just as the new kid on the block had better have a
gimmick, a scar, a great one-handed set shot, an uncle
on the cops. Youth seems to go after new sounds just
as it might new experiences. Perhaps the Manhattans
will have the word, know what it's all about. If not,
try Herman's Hermits, see what Ronny and the Day-
tonas have to say. Petula Clark will tell you that the
secret is to go downtown, that's where the lights are
bright. But maybe the Marvelettes have it and the
whole trouble is there are too many fish in the sea.
The Impressions tug at your elbow, tell you that faith
is the key, while Wayne Newton cautions against coming on too strong. One piece of advice all rock-'n'-
rollers accept with unanimity is Del Shannon's "You
got to keep searchin', searchin' . . . ."

The main life-giving fountains of rock 'n' roll are
the big city rock-'n'-roll stations, a key one being
WMCA in New York, programed in frenzied style,
each half second of the time accounted for, the music
and talk packed as tight as fruitcake ingredients.

It was WMCA that converted me to rock 'n' roll.
One day I drove to a car wash, the radio tuned in

to a "good-music" station, guaranteed to keep me corruption-free with plenty of Sinatra and Mantovani. Driving off later, I noticed that the dial had been turned, and I was listening to a sinful group called the Beatles singing "I Want to Hold Your Hand." It wasn't sinful. It was sweet, young, something pure about it. I drove on. The Dixiecups sang about going to the chapel. A girl named Dion Warwick very quietly broke my heart with "Walk On By," and that did it. I stayed in the car and listened for hours. A new kind of salted peanuts. It got so I could hardly wait to get into the car each morning to drive to the office.

In some fields, a pro is a man who plays hard, picks up his check, then couldn't care less about the sport until game time the next day. Not so in rock 'n' roll. Among the deejays, you sense a fevered, day-and-night commitment to the music. "This isn't background music, ever," Joe O'Brien of WMCA told me. "It's there in the foreground. You don't put it on and have yourself a pleasant chitchat. You listen, participate. It's arrogant, aggressive, positive, slaps you right in the face. You listen or turn it off."

There is plenty of opposition to rock 'n' roll, but to O'Brien, the hysterical pitch of the dissidents was due to a lack of effectiveness in their own lives. "But let's face it, you get two thousand kids screaming, half of the boys with hair down to their armpits, and they're a pain. So the adults forget about the music. It can be four kids singing an innocuous lyric about folks not understanding them, but it's the spectacle that's hard to take. The adult reaction becomes violent, irrational."

No matter what the starting point in rock-'n'-roll

talk, inevitably you must get around to the Beatles. To
O'Brien, they are wonderful composers, the best since
Irving Berlin. "And I Love Her," he predicted, would
become a standard, stay around for decades. "They
came along in the middle of a wave of songs constantly
stressing the negative. All of them had to do with a
guy calling a girl, and the girl is out. Then the Beatles
appeared, and suddenly everything worked out. 'I
Want to Hold Your Hand.' 'And I Love Her.' 'I'm
in Love with Her and I Feel Fine.' Suddenly, the girls
were always home. It wasn't Ringo's hair or John's
something or other. It was the approach of the music
itself. So many kids have told me that the Beatles made
them forget their grief over President Kennedy."

O'Brien thinks of rock 'n' roll as the first music
ever addressed directly to the vast teen-age world.

THE CALIFORNIA SOUND

Peter Bart

*There's the blues sound, the folk-rock sound, and the Detroit
sound. And in California they have a sound of their own called,
with neat deference to geography, the California sound. This is
rock 'n' roll set to lyrics describing the siren call of surfing at the
beach or the lure of automobile drag racing. Since California
living revolves around the beach and the automobile, some
admirers of the California sound claim that of all schools of
rock-'n'-roll music, it most nearly resembles authentic folk music.
Folk music or no, the California sound has earned millions for
a small group of its practitioners, the most notable of whom are
Jan and Dean. They even have the farm boys singing the praises
of Malibu Beach.*

California has long been credited with a number of
important contributions to the American way of life —
the outdoor-barbecue fetish, for example — but its role
as a cultural innovator has been underestimated. As
evidence, one need only turn to that contemporary
phenomenon known as the "California sound."

The California sound first came to national attention with the advent of surfing music — a curious fad
that spawned singing groups bearing such names as
the Beach Boys and the Fantastic Baggys (baggys are

the loose-fitting trunks worn by the surfing cult). Though the process of riding a surfboard over the breakers would seem to be, at best, a matter of purely coastal interest, surfing music quickly spread to the hinterland, and even the farm boys were soon singing the praises of the Malibu surf.

Since the rise of surfing music a couple of years ago, the California sound has undergone several metamorphoses. First there was the "sidewalk-surfing" phase that grew out of the popularity of the skateboard. The sidewalk-surfing music apparently assuaged the yearnings of the city youths who had to settle for pavements rather than ocean beneath their boards.

Next came the "carburetor-love-song" phase, in which the rock-'n'-roll troubadours expressed their undying devotion to their automobiles. Couched in hot-rod argot, replete with background drag-race noises, these numbers were all but unintelligible to anyone who didn't know, among other things, that "deuces" meant carburetors and "409" meant Chevrolet.

Out of these intimations of automania developed an even stranger phase: rock-'n'-roll tunes that related grisly tales of teen-age automobile accidents. The lyrics of these numbers offered morbid descriptions of bodies strewn across the road and limbs protruding out of windshields — all this while the Beatle beat kept hammering in the background.

Through all these changes, the exponents of the California sound have continued to expand their following. Some enthusiasts, in unguarded moments,

Jan & Dean

have even proclaimed that the California sound, alone among the various schools of rock-'n'-roll music, most nearly resembles authentic folk music, since its songs reflect the way of life of a region.

There is a kernel of truth to this contention. California living revolves around the automobile and the beach, and these are the subjects immortalized in the songs. The barely audible lyrics of the surfing songs reflect the surf addict's Spartan devotion to his board, a devotion that leaves little room for dalliance. Hence in a number titled, "Tell 'Em I'm Surfing," the lyrics tell how a cute little girl in the neighborhood who invited a boy to a poolside tryst gets put down for trying to distract her boyfriend from the rigors of the surf.

Similarly in the carburetor love songs, the car, not the girl, usually wins. In "Move Out Little Mustang," a boy with a Mustang (the Ford, not the horse) is crowded off the road by a pretty girl in a Thunderbird, so the boy does the chivalrous thing: he tries to crowd her off the road.

Most of the California-style rock-'n'-roll songs are composed by boys in their teens or early twenties, and they sound it. Each of the boys had his own specialty and is revered for his specialized know-how. For example, a twenty-four-year-old Los Angeles disc jockey, named Roger Christian, specializes in automobile songs; his reputation apparently derives more from his ability to find words to rhyme with "carburetor" than from any lyrical gift.

In the surfing (both seaside and sidewalk) specialty, two strapping young Californians, named Jan Berry and Dean Torrence ("Jan and Dean" to their followers) have established a certain hegemony, their recordings selling in the tens of millions. In some of their tunes, Jan and Dean have sought to escape from the sullen, self-consciousness of adolescent music by attempting to introduce a note of humor. Their albums are studded with tunes about little old ladies who have a penchant for drag racing. Hence "The Little Old Lady from Pasadena" is depicted as a granny with a heavy foot on the accelerator, and "meaner" too (to rhyme with "Pasadena").

Jan and Dean, blond, white, Anglo-Saxon, and middle-class, are eminently representative of California's rock-'n'-roll singers and set a vivid contrast to the ghetto-bound youths who dominate eastern rock-'n'-roll music. To the Easterners, rock 'n' roll is a way of life. Not to Jan and Dean. Between recording sessions and sojourns to the beach, Jan continues his studies at the California College of Medicine, while Dean studies fine arts at the University of Southern California. As Jan puts it, "We intend to be around earning a good living long after this surfing stuff has been forgotten."

Rock 'n' Roll Becomes Respectable

Louie Robinson

Its origins were humble. It started as the blues in southern plantation shacks and cotton fields, became rhythm and blues in big-city honky-tonks, and then, fused with western and country music, became rock 'n' roll, the teen-agers manna. Today rock 'n' roll has crossed the railroad tracks and become respectable. Not only does it account for most record sales, but housewives listen to it on the radio and, more recently, it has spawned TV shows with large adult as well as teen-age audiences. It has also created its own dances for which adults have flipped: the Monkey, Frug, Jerk, and Watusi. What better proof that rock 'n' roll has graduated to respectability than the fact that the Boston Pops Orchestra has recorded "I Want to Hold Your Hand"?

Twenty years ago, rock-'n'-roll music was only a gaudy sound in southern beer joints and on several hundred poorly waxed "race records." Today, rock-'n'-roll music has changed.

To the little old lady in Pasadena, the music may be a blasphemy on the name of Liberace. To a harassed housewife in a home full of transistor radios, it threatens to become the instrument of her eventual insanity. But to the nation's teen-agers, it's what's happening.

And therefore, for performers of the questionable art, both English and American, and including those Negroes who originated and perfected it and suffered it to be, it is now money in the bank.

Today, once lowly rock-'n'-roll music — that fusion of spirituals, blues, and even country and western sounds — is out of the honky-tonks and, praise be to television, into millions of living rooms and dens and bedrooms from Beverly Hills to Bogalusa. How did it get there?

The most listened-to radio stations in the country were all blaring with the sound of the big beat. In television land, somebody began to get the message. "We felt there had been no show that was really for the teen-agers and the kind of music they were listening to on radio," explains forty-four-year-old Dean Whitmore, producer of ABC-TV's "Shindig," the first of the current network rock-'n'-roll shows. It premièred in September, 1964. "We were also trying to say to adults, "This is what is going on now on the music scene," explains Whitmore, "and they did accept it. So our audience is not controlled entirely by teen-agers."

Indeed the audience is not solely nonadult. "Hullabaloo," the most successful show of the breed — albeit a hybrid between a rock-'n'-roll show and the "Ed Sullivan Show" — estimates that of its some 20,000,000 CBS-TV viewers the largest single group is adult women, numbering 7,250,000, and another 4,500,000 are men, with teen-agers and smaller children making up the rest.

As television has added sight to the sound, the sound itself has grown larger. In 1965, 127,000,000 — 90 per cent of the total — of the single records sold had the solid beat. Album sales added another $100,000,000 to the total, at a final cost of $580,000,000 to the public. Now, as it flows unendingly from juke boxes, TV, transistor sets, and car radios, in a river stretching from the United States to Britain to France to the Scandinavian countries, it seems as if the whole world has gone mad for the music.

What is this then that man, guitar, and drum have wrought? Well, it's hard to say exactly. For the music in its present state seems to defy intelligible definition. "It's the most versatile music without specific direction I've ever heard of," says Chuck Berry, one of the foremost exponents of the idiom. "It can be melancholy, happy, funny."

A onetime $14-a-night East St. Louis bistro performer, Berry now commands about $11,000 for a week's work. Of some 128 songs he has written, 118 of them were in the rock-'n'-roll vein. He has played Carnegie Hall, the Cow Palace, Las Vegas, and the Hollywood Palladium, and has made three trips to Europe. "There's hardly a performer in the business who doesn't owe something to Chuck Berry," declares one musical observer.

But even Berry, who is articulate about his art, can only approximate a definition of it. "Some of the beats — rhythm is actually what it is — are old gospel rhythm," Berry says. "The lyrics don't change through the years. It's still 'I love you, baby,' and things like that."

Whereas blues, a part of the ancestral strain of rock

Leadbelly

'n' roll, was twelve bars of music with three changes,
explains Berry, "Rock 'n' roll is not a progressive
music, it's an appreciative music. It's any music you can
dance by or exploit a particular story with. Take 'Roll
Over, Beethoven,' it's history actually." Berry wrote the
tune, and the Beatles took it and achieved unbelievable
fame and fortune. So much so that they are now, by
command of the Queen of England, Members of the
Order of the British Empire, and individual million-
aires. They have not done it without a bow in the direction of the source of their success. Said Beatle John
Lennon recently, "We can sing more colored than the
Africans."

The Beatles, of course, are not the only white performers to strike it rich with the brown sound. A prime
figure in the late fifties in moving rock 'n' roll to its
present pre-eminence in the music field, Elvis Presley is
now one of the highest paid actors in the world. Early
in his career, Presley talked of his youth in the South,
when he went to hear the old-time Negro gospel and
blues singers. Their effect on his styling is clear.

Other white performers currently doing extremely
well include the Righteous Brothers — Bill Medley and
Bob Hatfield, a pair of twenty-four-year-olds who on
sound alone would have to be accepted as Negroes.
Talking of how they teamed up, Medley declared
recently, "We both already had a colored sound. I
think that's why we got together." Even their name,
they say, came from the Negro expression "That's
Righteous, brother."

Thus while much else in the epic journey of rock-'n'-
roll music has changed, the sound was Negroid in the

beginning and it is to this day. The blues, born in the plantation shacks and cotton fields, and given voice by such men as Leadbelly and Blind Boy Fuller, met and blended with the gospel and spiritual chants, became jazz, spawned swing and bop, was carried to a new level with Ray Charles and his injection of the country and western flavor, made rich folk out of Fats Domino, Chubby Checker, and the Supremes.

For at least ten years now, people have been predicting that rock 'n' roll, like Shakespeare's poor player, would strut and fret its hour upon the stage and then be gone. Yet it persists and probably will, either as rock 'n' roll (as the late disc jockey Alan Freed dubbed it originally) or as pop rock or rockabilly or one of the half-dozen names variously attached to it. Jimmy O'Neil, host of the "Shindig" show, sees the trend "getting toward a very deep intellectual meaning in the lyrics." Says he, "This is the thing that bothers me. We're now getting to real dismal things like 'Eve of Destruction.' I'd like to see us get back to more hopeful themes."

But morbid, funny, or intellectual, the lyrics for the rock-'n'-roller seem of only minor concern. The beat is the thing. And, as John Philip Sousa once said of jazz, it "will endure just as long as people hear it through their feet instead of their brains." The only problem is that Sousa erred slightly: people now hear jazz with their brains perhaps most of all, and it has achieved new heights of popularity. But if rock 'n' roll, with its heavy beat and nerve-tugging twangs and rhythmic grunts, ever invades the brain, the future indeed seems perilous.

Yet all may not be lost, "Shindig" producer Whitmore points out. "There is a lot of bad rock-'n'-roll music, but if you get into it, you find that some of it has some very good construction." As evidence he points to the recording of the Beatle hit "I Want to Hold Your Hand" by Arthur Fiedler and the Boston Pops Orchestra.

From plantation shack to the Boston Pops is definitely a success story.

2.
WHO?

Songs and Singers

How does a rock-'n'-roll song become a hit? It starts with a songwriter selling his tune to a music publisher. Step Number 2, a singer or a vocal group records it. Step Number 3, a disc jockey plays it, or it is performed live on television. On the next pages are stories about a husband-and-wife songwriting team, Cynthia Weil and Barry Mann, who have produced such hits as "Home of the Brave," "You've Lost That Lovin' Feeling," and "We Gotta Get Out of This Place"; the Supremes, a trio of Detroit girls who have five gold records (each has sold 1,000,000 copies or more) to their credit, including "Where Did Our Love Go?" "Baby Love," and "Come See About Me"; Doug Henderson, a fast-talking, hit-predicting TV disc jockey better known as Jocko; and Lada Edmund, Jr., the girl who does those kooky rock-'n'-roll dances in a cage on the "Hullabaloo" TV show.

The Songwriters

Norma Sue Woodstone

Once upon a time, rock 'n' roll was a beat and a melody that could stand alone. The lyrics didn't matter so much. But the latest word is "message" music. It's

music that's for a cause, music that's for or against
something — anything, everything.

Cynthia Weil and Barry Mann, husband-and-wife
songwriting team, have recently zoomed to fame and
fortune with their best-selling "messages." She writes
the lyrics; he writes the music.

"We feel that our songs say something," Barry says.
"For example, we have a song against using dope coming out soon. But we don't just start out to write a
'message' song. First we have to feel strongly about a
cause — something that we think needs straightening
out. Then we try to put the idea into exciting music."

Cynthia, twenty-four, and Barry, twenty-six, have
worked together for four years. "I always thought I
would be a performer," Cynthia says. "I wanted to be
an actress, a dancer, or a singer. After I graduated from
college, I had a part on a TV show. But then I discovered I was more interested in writing lyrics than in acting. So I got a job in the music business."

Barry hadn't planned to be a songwriter, either. "I
went to college and studied architecture for a year and
a half," he says. "But I dropped out to learn more
about the music field. I studied music for three years
when I was a child. That's all the music studying I ever
did."

Cynthia and Barry met at a music company. She was
writing lyrics for a singer, and he was writing music.
"My song ended up on the back of his, and we ended
up married," Cynthia says.

How do they go about writing a song? "It varies,"
Cynthia says. "Sometimes he has a tune first. Sometimes
I have a title or a story to tell first. Then he looks over

my work and makes suggestions. We work well together."

Cynthia and Barry have had six best sellers within the past year. Their annual income is now $100,000. Some of their hits are Eydie Gormé's "Blame It on the Bossa Nova," the Righteous Brothers' "You've Lost That Lovin' Feeling," and the Animals' "We Gotta Get Out of This Place." One of their most popular "message" songs is "Home of the Brave." They have also written songs for Steve Lawrence, Bobby Rydell, the Drifters, James Darren, the Crystals, Jody Miller, and for three TV shows.

"You'd think it would get easier and easier for us to write songs," Cynthia says. "But lately it's taken us longer to write a song than it used to. It's because we are both more critical now. Sometimes a song just comes out, and other times it takes forever."

"Even after we've written a song, we still keep working on it," Barry says. "Sometimes we cut a record over and over again until we're satisfied."

What is the most important part of a rock-'n'-roll song? "I write the lyrics, so I like to think they're important," Cynthia says. "I like for them to say something. Kids seem to think the lyrics are important, too. A lot of them are buying magazines that print the words of hit songs. They want to know the words. Then again, take a song like 'Hang on, Sloopy.' Those lyrics don't say anything. But the repetition of the words is catchy, and it's a good record to dance to."

"You have to take each song individually," Barry says. "In protest songs, like P. F. Sloan's 'Eve of Destruction,' the words are important for the record to be a hit. The feeling of the words is also important — the idea, what the song is trying to say. Then, in some songs you can't even understand the lyrics, but it doesn't matter. The most important things are the melody, the *idea* of the lyrics, the sound of the singers and instruments. Good rock 'n' roll is a happy blending of all these things."

Why do they think rock 'n' roll caught on so well with teen-agers? "It's something that's theirs," Cynthia says. "The singers are young, the writers are young, the producers are young."

"And the feeling's theirs, too," Barry says.

THE SUPREMES

Barbara Altshuler

Who's the supreme singing hit in the United States today? You've got it! The Supremes! They have spread the "Detroit sound" — a combination of rock 'n' roll, rhythm 'n' blues, gospel, and pop — across the country. Today, it's sweeping Europe and giving the Beatles competition on their own home ground.

Diana Ross, twenty-one, Florence Ballard, twenty-two, and Mary Wilson, twenty-two, are the first American pop-singing group to have five Number 1 hit records in a row. They are also the first all-girl group to head the British record polls. Together, they made more than $500,000 in 1965.

The Supremes

All this would have seemed unbelievable six years ago, when they were three Detroit high school girls. Diana went to Cass Technical High, and Mary and Florence went to Northeastern High. They got together during their spare time and harmonized, wherever they could — while walking, in each other's homes, in the community center near the Brewster-Douglas housing projects. Their neighborhood, they say, had three things: rats, roaches, and — happily — music.

"We started singing what was popular and what we could sing," Mary says. "We found that our voices blended." Soon they were singing at parties, dances, and programs in the community. Meanwhile they studied music in school and sang at church.

The girls were "discovered" in 1960 by a talent scout while singing at a record hop one night in the neighborhood community center. His company: Motown, a new record company that was looking for young singers. Motown president Berry Gordy listened to them, but turned them down. He thought they were too young. "Come back and see me when you finish high school," he told them. A year later, after graduating, the girls went back to Motown. This time they signed a contract.

Next came hours of rehearsals and recording sessions. They made nine records. They waited three years for one to click. Meanwhile they worked — in a department store, in a record shop, babysitting.

Finally, in June, 1964, the Supremes recorded their tenth song, "Where Did Our Love Go?" It clicked — big. It has sold 2,000,000 copies. The Supremes have since had four more "gold" records (sales of 1,000,000 or more).

The girls describe their sound as "blues with a pop beat." Diana sings the lead, while Mary supplies the alto and Florence the soprano. "We try not to sound like anyone else," they say. "Too often a group gets a hit record and then everyone else tries to imitate them. That's the reason so many records sound alike. Too many people try to imitate rather than create."

Money and fame have not spoiled the Supremes. Their first thought, when the money started coming in, was of their families. They moved them out of the projects and into large, pretty homes. Out of their earnings, each girl draws $100 a week for herself. Most of this goes for clothes. They always dress alike when onstage, and sometimes offstage too. "We've been dressing alike since our high school days," Diana says. "We don't intend to change the pattern now. Things are going too well."

What are their plans for the future? "We'll keep singing together as long as the public listens," Diana says. "But we know it won't last forever. We're reaching teen-agers now because they like our sound. We realize that one day they'll turn to someone else." When that happens, Diana wants to go to college. "We learn a lot about life from being on the road," she says. "But that's not enough by itself. You need book education too." Mary and Florence both want marriage and children.

What advice would the Supremes give to teen-agers, "Stay in school," they say. "So many youngsters want to plunge into show business and try to make it big. But they can't all be as lucky as we've been. It's much better to get that sheepskin first. After all, we did."

JOCKO THE DJ

Joyce Jenkins

Who's the ace from outer space. It's Jocko!

Doug Henderson walked into a radio station in Baltimore, Maryland, thirteen years ago. He got a job as a disc jockey and called himself "Jocko."

"I worked seven weeks for zero pay," he says. "The station director said the experience would be more valuable than the money."

Today Jocko owns half of radio station WIKI in Richmond, Virginia. Until recently he taped shows for stations in seven big cities. He now has his own daily TV show, "Jocko's Rocket Ship Show" (on a UHF station in the New York area).

Why the outer-space bit? "I catch the hit records before they reached earth," Jocko says. "I mean I predict *future* hits each week." Jocko sends his predictions, by request, to radio stations, record companies, and other DJ's. Some time ago Jocko predicted that these records would be "big, bad, and boss": "I Got You" ("I Feel Good"), James Brown; "Seesaw," Don Covay; "Up Tight," Little Stevie Wonder. (He was right.)

Jocko's specialty is "soul" music. "That's music that creates a moving feeling within you," he says. "It makes you feel a part of what you're listening to. It reaches out to *your* soul. It can be anything — rock 'n' roll, jazz, pop, classical — but mostly it's rhythm and blues."

What's Jocko's advice to teen-agers who want to be disc jockeys? "Get at least a high-school education," he says. "A DJ needs good English and a quick mind. We don't follow a script. We just talk. And DJ's try to create an original style — something that will give us identification." (Have you ever listened to Jocko? If you're not with it, he'll lose you — fast.)

"A DJ's job sounds glamorous," says Jocko. "But when you face that mike day after day, some of the glamour wears off. It's work, like any other job. But I wouldn't trade it."

HULLABALOO GIRL

Norma Sue Woodstone

Do you know who Lada Edmund, Jr., is? No? Okay. Have you ever seen the kooky blond dancer in the cage on "Hullabaloo"? *That's* Lada Edmund, Jr.

Lada has also played in a Broadway musical, made a movie, appeared on three TV variety shows, done TV commercials, written a national gossip column, and modeled. Show-business experts guess that she makes between $20,000 and $25,000 a year. She is eighteen years old.

How did Lada become a top dancer and a TV star? "Back home in Minneapolis, Minnesota, I used to play a lot of football," she says. "I was such a clod that my mother decided to send me to ballet classes. The other girls walked into class carrying their toe shoes. I carried my football."

Lada was five then. Three years later, in New York City, she switched from ballet to jazz dancing. She has studied jazz dancing ever since.

"When I first did 'Hullabaloo,'" she says, "everyone figured I could do all the steps. But I couldn't. So when the other kids on the show did the steps, I just exaggerated what they did. They thought I was great. Then I got the cage thing. Now I'm *the* rock-'n'-roll dancer. When I'm up in the cage, I just do what I want to do. Sometimes I do something of my own up there, and later I see kids doing it in discothèques."

Lada often goes dancing "just for fun" after she has practiced all day for a show. "You can't really unwind when you dance on a show," she says. "I don't smoke or drink. So I go out dancing to unwind. I don't have any favorite dances. I do them all. Anything with a beat — rock 'n' roll, Billie Holiday, Glenn Miller."

Why does Lada think rock 'n' roll is so popular? "It has a feeling of something coming, rather than something that's been," she says. "And it's a *moving* situation. Good music, like Brahms, you can sit and listen to that. But I couldn't see sitting and listening to the Beach Boys."

MUSIC'S GOLD BUGS: THE BEATLES

Alfred G. Aronowitz

They wore Edwardian suits that were too small for them, high-heeled boots, and had manes of shaggy hair. When they arrived in New York in February, 1964, thousands of teen-age girls besieged them. It was the same story everywhere they went. These were the Beatles, up from poverty in Liverpool, now monarchs of the world of rock-'n'-roll. There were dozens of rock-'n'-roll groups in the United States that could sing better and play better than the Beatles, but there was this difference: while American rock 'n' roll groups sang dirgelike laments for lost love, the Beatles were fun and upbeat. Refusing to take themselves seriously, they sang "I Want to Hold Your Hand," "And I Love Her," "I'm in Love with Her and I Feel Fine." Their brand of the big beat made converts of millions.

Brian Sommerville is a balding thirty-two-year-old Londoner whose jaw juts out like the southeast corner of England when he thinks he is about to say something important. At Kennedy International Airport in New York on February 7, 1964, Sommerville's jaw was projecting so far he was almost unable to open his mouth to speak. A thousand screaming teen-agers were trying to wriggle toward a thin white line of a nylon rope that had been stretched across the terminal building lobby. Three thousand more were screaming from behind bulging metal railings atop the roof, where they were the guests of New York disc jockeys, who had invited them to take the day off from school.

Next to Sommerville a New York *Journal-American* photographer was tugging angrily at his arm, shouting, "We bought an exclusive story, and we can't even get a picture of them looking at us — what did we pay you money for?" At Sommerville's other arm a phalanx of British correspondents was complaining that the police wouldn't let them into the pressroom. There wasn't space left in the pressroom anyway, and one of the cops tried to throw out a Capitol Records executive who had arrived without an identification badge. Disc jockeys equipped with tape recorders were pointing cylindrical microphones at the mob. Flashbulbs exploded. From the back of the lobby came word that two girls had fainted. Hemmed in and harassed, Sommerville's jaw signaled a pronouncement. "This," he said in the intonations of a nation that has been accustomed to ruling the world, "has gotten entirely out of control." Sommerville is press officer of a rock-'n'-roll group known as the Beatles. Their plane had just landed.

Amid a fanfare of screeches, there emerged four young Britons in Edwardian four-button suits. One was short and thick-lipped. Another was handsome and peach-fuzzed. A third had a heavy face and the hint of buckteeth. On the fourth, the remnants of adolescent pimples were noticeable. Their names were Ringo Starr, Paul McCartney, John Lennon, and George Harrison, but they were otherwise indistinguishable beneath their manes of moplike hair.

After they were ushered into the floodlit uproar of

the pressroom, Brian Sommerville, acting as master of ceremonies, stepped to a microphone, again thrust out his jaw, and addressed the reporters. "Gentlemen, gentlemen, gentlemen," he said, "will you please shut up!" The first question from the American press was, "Do you believe in lunacy?" "Yeah," answered one of the Beatles, "it's healthy." Another reporter asked, "Would you please sing something?" "No," replied another Beatle, "we need money first." Still another reporter asked, "Do you hope to take anything home with you?" "Yeah," a Beatle replied, "Rockefeller Center." At first, few of the reporters could remember which Beatle was which. But by the end of their two-week visit to America, each of them had become a distinct personality. Each of them, in fact, had become a star.

Ringo is the one that some observers have compared to Harpo Marx. He has bright-blue eyes that remind one of a child looking through a window, although he sometimes deliberately crosses them as he sits dumbly at the drums, playing his corny four-four beat. "I hate phonies," he says with the absolutism of somebody who thinks he can spot one a mile away. "I can't *stand* them." The most popular of the Beatles in America, he evokes paroxysms of teen-age shrieks everywhere by a mere turn of his head, a motion which sends his brown spaniel hair flying. When he flips his wig, the kids flip theirs. "Riiinngo! Riinngo!" the kids call out. He acquired the nickname because he wears two rings on each hand. He wears different rings at different times, changing them like cuff links. "I like the gold ones," he says. "The fans send a lot of silver ones too, but I send them back." Then he adds, "Do you know I have 2,761 rings?" His fame has brought Ringo other treasures, but he seems not to have forgotten what it was like to grow up amid the grimy row-house streets of Liverpool.

He was born Richard Starkey, the only son of a father who was a house painter and a mother who was a barmaid. He never finished school. He was kept out by pleurisy and more than a dozen stomach operations. Also, it seems, he never started growing. Asked how tall he is, he snaps back, "Two feet, nine inches!" Actually he is five feet seven. "When I feel my head starting to swell," says John Lennon, "I just look at Ringo and I know perfectly well we're not supermen." Without proper schooling, Ringo worked as an electrician's apprentice and at various odd jobs before turning to drumming.

"When I was sixteen, you know," he says, "I used to walk on the road with the rest of the lot and we'd have all our drape coats on and we'd have a few laughs with the rival gangs, and then I got the drums and the bloke next door and I got a job and we started playing together, and another bloke and me made a bass out of an old tea chest and this was about 1958, mind you, and we played together and then we started playing on dances and things, you know, and we took an interest in it and we stopped going out and hanging around corners every night."

These days still lie close behind him. When an American reporter asked him if he liked fish and chips, he answered, "Yes, I like fish and chips, but I like steak and chips better." One of his greatest moments was when the Beatles played before Princess Margaret and the Queen Mother at the Royal Command Performance

Beatles after receiving decorations from Queen Elizabeth.

in London last November. "It was the first time I ever
felt British," he says. "You know, you never think
about royalty. But the Queen Mother, she was a nice
lady."

He sits with his drums behind the group as the
other three perform, and he rarely sings, although
that is what he would most like to do. At twenty-five
he is the oldest of the Beatles, but he is at the bottom
of what sociologists would call their pecking order.
When he joined the group it already had a record contract, and the unspoken feeling in the quartet is that
Ringo was hired by the other three. When they dis-
agree on anything, Ringo is the last to get his way.
"You'd be nowhere," Paul McCartney says to him in
the ultimate squelch, "if it weren't for the rest of us."

The fans call Paul the handsome one, and he knows
it. The others in the group call Paul "The Star." He
does most of the singing and most of the wiggling,
trying to swing his hips after the fashion of Elvis
Presley, one of his boyhood idols. In the British equiva-
lent of high school, Paul was mostly in the upper ranks
scholastically, unlike the other Beatles. "He was like,
you know, a goody-goody in school," remembers one
of Paul's boyhood friends. He also, as another former
classmate remembers him, was a "tubby little kid" who
avoided girlish rejections by avoiding girls.

Paul, who plays bass guitar, wears the same tight
pants that are part of the uniform of the Beatles, although he often distinguishes himself by a vest. "Paul,"
says one member of the troupe, "is the only one of the
boys who's had it go to his head." Sometimes, talking
with the other Beatles, he finds himself using accents
much more high-toned than the working-class slang

of Liverpool, where he grew up. When he does, John
Lennon mockingly mimics him.

Paul and John have collaborated in writing more
than 100 songs, including such hits as "I Want to Hold
Your Hand" and "She Loves You." "None of us really
knows how to read or write music," says Paul. "The
way we work it is like: just whistling. John will whistle
at me, and I'll whistle back at him."

John doesn't smile when he sings. "That's because,"
says Neil Aspinall, the twenty-two-year-old road manager who grew up in Liverpool with the Beatles, "he's
giving you his soul." He likes to wear sunglasses both
indoors and out, as a sort of declaration of privacy.
"John," says Brian Epstein, the twenty-nine-year-old
personal manager who discovered the Beatles, "is the
most intellectual of the boys." Though he has a habit
of falling asleep at odd moments, he is also the most
intense and has a temper that reddens his face at the
slightest rub. At a cocktail party in the British embassy
after the Beatles' Washington concert, John found himself besieged by dignitaries, their wives and girlfriends,
all of whom were thrusting autograph books at him
with such official commands as, "Look, sign this for
my daughter! Cawn't think why she likes you! Must
be out of her mind." Finally John pushed away the
pens. Forcing his way to the bar, he ordered a drink
and said, "These people are worse than the fans. These
people have no bloody manners. Now, the Ambassa-
dor, I liked him; we talk the same language. But I
wouldn't give a thank you for his friends." At that
moment a young embassy official approached John and
said, "Come now and do your stuff." John glared back.
"I'm not going back through that crowd — I want a

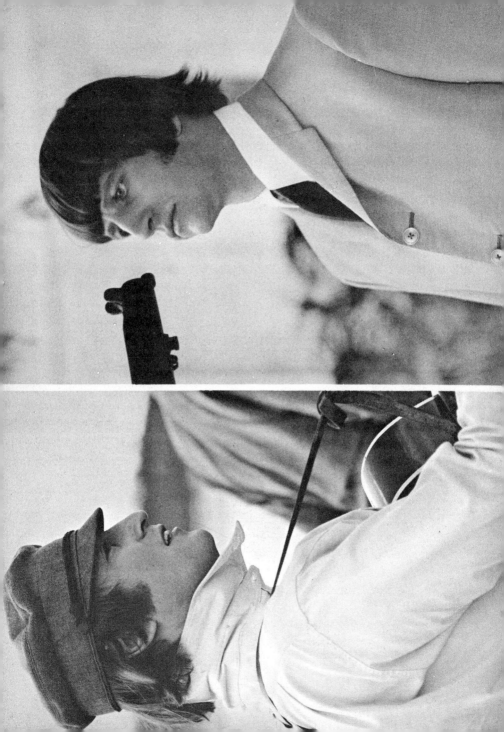

drink," he said. "Oh yes you are," the official said
imperiously. Livid, John turned to Ringo and said,
"I'm getting out of here!" With a smile, Ringo put an
arm on John's shoulder and said calmly, "Oh come on,
let's get it over with." The "stuff" consisted of draw-
ing names out of a box in a charity raffle.

John began with ideas of becoming a painter, spending two years at the Liverpool Art Institute. He also
writes short stories and poems, a collection of which,
combined with his sketches, is being published in London. He has since written two books, *In His Own
Write* and *A Spaniard in the Works.* One editor calls
Lennon's literary efforts "British hip, a sort of con-
glomeration of funny Lewis Carroll jabberwocky and
an almost Joycean word play."

When John first appeared on the "Ed Sullivan
Show," a subtitle identifying him carried the paren-
thetical message, "Sorry, girls, he's married." His wife
Cynthia is a quietly beautiful twenty-one-year-old
blonde whom he met at the Liverpool Art Institute
and whom the newspapers now call, to the Lennons'
disgust, "Mrs. Beatle." When the Beatles traveled from
New York to Washington, she wore a black wig so
she could get through the crowd. In Washington, she
remained alone in her hotel room. In Miami Beach,
she sunbathed by herself. "Ever since the boys became
famous," says Cynthia, "it's become more and more
difficult for me to see John." They have an infant son,
John, whom the newspapers call, again to their disgust, "Baby Beatle." When the Lennons have business
visitors, Cynthia serves tea and recedes into the background.

John is the leader of the Beatles. "We *have* no

leader," he might argue with some annoyance. "We're
a *team*, y' know, pull together and all that." As a
matter of fact, each Beatle has a veto on what the four
of them do together. "But it's John who usually wins
out," says one of their friends. "John is the hippest
and the sharpest of the lot. They've all learned from
him. Even their humor, the way they're always sending
people up, they got that from John."

Just twenty-three, George Harrison is the youngest
of the Beatles. "He doesn't have the maturity of the
others, so he tends to play it a little safe," says a member of the troupe. "It's as if he's the baby of the
family." Being the baby of the family is a role to which
George is accustomed. The son of a bus driver, he is
the youngest of four children. "George was always the
one who tried to please," says his sister, Mrs. Louise
Caldwell, the pretty platinum-blond wife of an engineer who lives in the Midwest. "When the fire needed
more coal, he would always say, 'Mummy, I'll do it.
Let me get the shovel.' Or when we'd be going to
church, George would polish everyone's boots."

George plays lead guitar for the Beatles, often with
a look of unconcern that seems to reflect a desire to
be strumming elsewhere. "Well," he says, "the songs
that Paul and John write, they're all right, but they're
not the greatest."

His boyhood idols were guitarists Chet Atkins and
Duane Eddy, although he recently discovered Andres
Segovia. He listens on the radio to other pop artists
from the start of his day, which often begins when
road manager Aspinall drags the boys out of bed at
10:30 to keep some 10 A.M. date. He keeps a transistor radio in his hand, even during conversations. He

adjusts the volume according to his interest in what is being said.

"You have to be very careful of what you say to George," says disc jockey Murray (the K) Kaufman of New York's WINS, who glad-handed the Beatles when they stepped off the plane in New York and who was George's roommate when the Beatles traveled to Miami Beach. "You have to be sure that every word means what you want it to mean. He takes what you say very literally."

"George, as a matter of fact," says manager Brian Epstein, "is the only one who asks questions. He's the only one who takes an active interest in the business aspect of the Beatles. He wants to know how I book them, how the discs are distributed, and everything that has to do with the financial workings."

George's ambition, he says, is to retire with "a whacking great pile of money." He recalls that in the early days of the group in Liverpool, "we got what would work out to two dollars a night apiece — and all the soda we could drink. We drank until that stuff came out of our ears, to make sure we got our money's worth."

Although by no means the quietest of the Beatles, because none of them really is quiet, George remains the least prominent. At a press conference for fan magazines in New York's Plaza Hotel, a young woman asked, "Mr. Starr is known for his rings, Mr. McCartney obviously for his looks, and Mr. Lennon for his wife. What about you, Mr. Harrison?" George swallowed a bite of a chicken sandwich, fluttered his long eyelashes in the same manner that Paul often does, and answered, "As long as I get an equal share of the money, I'm willing to stay anonymous."

These are the Beatles — the four young men who brought with them to America a phenomenon known as Beatlemania. So far, Beatlemania has traveled over two continents. In Stockholm, the arrival of the Beatles was greeted with teen-age riots. In Paris, another congregation held screeching services at the airport and the Beatles' performances at the Olympia Theater were sold out for three weeks. In the Beatles' native Liverpool, sixty youngsters collapsed from exposure after standing all night in a mile-long line of 12,000 waiting to buy tickets to the Beatles' performance. When a foreman shut off the radio in the middle of a Beatles record at a textile mill in Lancashire, 200 girls went out on strike.

While the Beatles toured the United States, three of their singles were in the top six and their albums ranked one and two in the record-popularity charts. Beatle wigs were selling at three dollars apiece, high-school boys were combing their forelocks forward, and hairdressers were advertising Beatle cuts for women. Beatle hats, T-shirts, cookies, eggcups, ice cream, dolls, beach shirts, turtleneck pullovers, nighties, socks, and iridescent blue-and-green collarless suits were on the market, and a Beatle motor scooter for children and a Beatlemobile for adults were being readied for production. "I think everyone has gone daft," says John. Adds Ringo, "Anytime you spell 'beetle' with an 'a' in it, we get the money." In 1964, Beatle-licensed products grossed $50,000,000 in America alone. As for the Beatles, their total income that year reached $14,000,000.

It all began in Liverpool, a smog-aired, dockfront city that overlooks the Mersey River. When the Beatles first put their brows together eight years ago, there were an estimated 100 rock-'n'-roll groups in the city. Today Liverpool is the pop-music capital of the British Isles, and what newspapers have come to call "the Mersey sound" dominates the English hit parade. "Do you want to know what the Mersey sound is?" says one American critic. "It's 1956 American rock bouncing back at us."

In the beginning, the group was called the Quarrymen Skiffle Group, then the Moondogs, and then the Moonshiners. John, Paul, and George were in the original group; Ringo Starr joined in 1962. Hired in 1959 for a job in Hamburg, Germany, the Beatles worked their way up to a wage of $25 a week, and became one of the main attractions along the Reeperbahn.

"When they got back to Liverpool, that's when they really started to swing," says Neil Aspinall. It was then that Brian Epstein discovered them. A delicately mannered young man who once wanted to be a dress designer, Epstein at the time was in charge of the television-radio-records department of his father's department-store chain. When several customers began demanding Beatle records, Epstein signed them up, got them a test with Decca Records (they flunked), then brought them to Electric and Musical Industries, Ltd.

"They were impressive — it was like striking oil," recalls an E.M.I. official. "I remember I gave them back their first tape and told them, 'If there's anything you don't like, let me know.' And George came right back and said, 'Well, I don't like your tie for a start.'"

In short order the Beatles had four hits, and teen-age mobs began following the Beatles throughout England. But it wasn't until they played London's Palladium and several thousand fans mobbed them that the Beatles became national heroes. They had to be rescued by police. "Well, there were no assassinations that day," recalls Brian Sommerville. "There were no wars, no invasions, no great crises of state, and the Beatles were the only good story the London dailies had, so they gave it a big display."

In the United States, Capitol Records, which has first rights to any E.M.I. release, originally turned down the Beatles' records. As the craze grew, it not only issued them but poured $50,000 into a promotion campaign. "Sure there was a lot of hype," says Capitol vice-president Voyle Gilmore. "But all the hype in the world isn't going to sell a bad product."

Nevertheless, that hype helped stir the interest of thousands of fans who greeted the Beatles at Kennedy Airport. Many thousands more waited for them at New York's Plaza Hotel. Outside the hotel, stacked up against barricades, the mob chanted, "We want the Beatles! We want the Beatles!" According to one maid, the Beatles found three girls hiding in their bathtub. Dozens of others climbed the fire exit to the twelfth-floor wing in which the Beatle entourage had been ensconced. Still others, with the names and pocketbooks of prominent families, checked in at the hotel and tried to get to the Beatles via the elevators.

On the twelfth floor the Beatles rested in their suite, while the phones rang with requests for interviews and autographs. One call was from a man who wanted to produce Beatle ash trays. Another was from a promoter in Hawaii who wanted to book the Beatles.

Telegrams came in by the handful, and boxes loaded with fan mail. "We get 12,000 letters a day," Ringo later said. "Yeah," added John. "We're going to answer every one of them." The road managers, meanwhile, were busy signing the Beatles' autographs for them, and the room-service waiters kept bringing up tables loaded with all sorts of drinks. Murray the K also came in, bringing with him the Ronettes, an American recording group of three exotic-looking girls. "We met the Beatles in Europe," one of them said, as if she were singing it.

As the Beatles' stay at the Plaza extended, so did the throngs. Each time the Beatles left the hotel, the mobs would break through police lines in a jumble of lost shoes, falling girls, and Beatle sweat shirts. A deputy chief inspector of police accused the Beatles' press agents of bringing in teen-agers by the busload. The Beatles, meanwhile, spent their time watching TV, dining at the 21 Club, sightseeing from their car, twisting at the Peppermint Lounge, and flirting with waitresses.

The remainder of the Beatles' tour of America was more of the same. In Washington, to which the Beatles traveled aboard a private railroad car called the "King George," 2,000 teen-age fans mobbed the locked metal gates of Union Station. At their concert in the Coliseum that night the Beatles were showered with flashbulbs, hair rollers, caramels, and jelly beans, in some instances a bagful at a time. "They *hurt*," Ringo said afterward. "They felt just like hailstones."

When they flew to Miami, they were greeted at the airport by a chimpanzee, four bathing beauties, a four-mile-long traffic jam, and 7,000 teen-agers, who shattered twenty-three windows and a plate-glass door. The flight engineer of the plane wore a Beatle wig. As they were getting off, the wife of the president of National Airlines came aboard with two teen-age girls, but was blocked by Sommerville, who stormed, "No, no, madam! We cannot spend time giving autographs to employees' families."

After their American tour, the Beatles flew back to England to make their first movie. When they stopped off at Kennedy Airport to change planes for London, they again found several thousand teen-age fans screaming from the observation roof, after waiting there for hours. Four girls collapsed. When it was all over, America relaxed again.

ELVIS—
TEN MILLION DOLLARS LATER
Vernon Scott

When in 1956 he made his national television debut, Elvis Presley struck most parents as an emissary of the devil. Hair hanging in his face, hips undulating like a stripteaser's, his voice hoarse with emotion, he outraged adult sensibilities. But the more parents, moralists, clergymen, and critics railed against him, the more teen-agers flipped for him. Elvis was for them the supreme symbol of juvenile rebellion. Today, ten years later, Elvis is a more subdued performer, but his genius still lies in his ability to communicate with adolescents. Young people realize that he is one of them and that he belongs to them. To them he is a teen-age dream come true, a modern Peter Pan in Never-Never Land.

The M-G-M guard waved his hand in recognition as a black Rolls-Royce bearing Tennessee license plates and a white Chrysler station wagon swept through the studio's east gate and rolled to a halt outside an imposing dressing room. The doors of the cars opened simultaneously, to disgorge nine hatless young men in dark clothes, who moved with practiced ease, almost like Secret Service men guarding the President. The nine indeed were on guard duty — escort duty, they prefer to say — on a scale not seen in Hollywood even in the days of Valentino and Fairbanks, Sr. And the man they were escorting, obviously a film star, was the next to disembark. An adult might have wondered who it was that required this kind of almost military protection. But probably any teen-ager in the country would instantly have recognized the idol, Elvis Presley.

A youthful, strapping 175-pounder, with dark, shiny hair, pale and sensuous features, and an easy smile, Presley made his way forthwith to the sound stage, took the leading lady's chin in his hand and drawled, "Mornin'," then stood respectfully at attention to say, "Good morning, sir," in a different tone of voice, to the director.

Elvis Presley, the guitarist and singing performer whose singing style created a national hubbub in the mid-1950's, was generally expected to go into permanent decline when he was drafted into Army service in 1958. But that's not what happened. Unless you are a dedicated Presley fan, you may be surprised to learn that since leaving the Army in 1960, Elvis has starred in seventeen movies — four times as many as he made during the pre-Army headline period. What's more, all the pictures have made money at the box office, and Elvis' current headquarters on the M-G-M lot are the fabled Dressing Room A, once the domain of the late Clark Gable.

It is almost as if Elvis had gone underground since returning to civilian life. The public screaming has subsided, but the passions are still aroused, and Presley is still an American legend in the select subworld of the very young, the adolescent, the nonadult. At thirty-one, he may well be the top money earner in show business: $600,000 per picture, plus a percentage of the profits; an estimated $200,000 per year (conservatively) from the sale of phonograph records; royalties from the sale of Elvis Presley T-shirts, Presley rings, and the like. His gross income is estimated at $2,000,000 per year, and it's fairly safe to guess that his take so far has totaled in substantial excess of $10,000,000.

Time has wrought a few differences in Elvis. The deep sideburns have been cropped. There has been some modification of the extreme zoot-suit flair of dress, and a moderate toning down of the bumps and grinds. The latter, although still in doubtful taste, have become less startling in these days of the Twist.

But Presley's old mob appeal is unmistakably there. Only a few months ago, when Elvis made one of his rare ventures into public view, several dozen policemen were needed to keep the crowd from crushing him in an effort to get autographs and tear buttons from his clothes. It is this adoration by fans that has provided him with more money in hand than he ever had seen, and Elvis today is displaying a bizarre way of spending it that baffles and intrigues even Hollywood.

Still a bachelor, he owns Graceland, the Memphis estate he bought for his parents in 1957; leases a tremendous white Mediterranean-style home in the exclusive Bel-Air section of Los Angeles; has eleven automobiles, at last count, including a $30,000 Cadillac with innumerable extras (among them special carpeting, a hi-fi phonograph with six stereo speakers, a public-address system, to convey Presley's greetings to surprised pedestrians, and a television set in the back

Elvis Presley

seat); and is the sole support of a retinue of from seven to twelve hangers-on, mostly from Tennessee, who live with him, form what appears to be both bodyguard and his only circle of friends.

But Elvis doesn't drink, smoke, or swear, rarely goes to night clubs or restaurants, has practically no hobbies, doesn't insult people, doesn't get arrested, doesn't get into fights or other public trouble, and shows no inclination whatever to mix with other movie people (except, occasionally, to date the leading lady of his current movie).

His nonworking hours are passed chiefly in watching television, playing records, romping through touch football with his cohorts, and generally "hanging around" with the crowd from Tennessee. He has a few dates with Hollywood actresses; more often, though, the dates are unknown girls. Where he goes and what he does on these dates, nobody but the principals seem to know, and they aren't saying. Elvis himself turns away all questions with the comment, "Heck, I shouldn't be talking about things like that. That information ought to come from the girls."

Through relentless effort on the part of his manager, Tom Parker, and the publicity departments of various studios for which he has worked, Presley's "image" has emerged today as a clean-cut introvert, humble and thus almost without personality. They'd have you believe he is a phantom. (Detractors label him a hick with money.) Elvis has achieved a neutral personality, a haven from his early and horrendous image as a stomp-and-holler sex symbol for female adolescents. And it is this transformation that has saved him from obscurity.

If a good many adults had had their way, the Presley career would have come to an end in 1956, when he made his national television debut with the late Jimmy and Tommy Dorsey on their network show. Hair hanging in his face, hips undulating, and voice hoarse with emotion, Presley beamed into millions of living rooms as some special emissary of the devil, in the minds of parents seeing him for the first time. Successive appearances, with Milton Berle and Ed Sullivan, swelled the cry to a national storm of protest. But the more determined parents grew to expel Elvis from decent society, the greater grew teen devotion.

Moralists accused him of corrupting the nation's youth. Clergymen railed against him. Columnists coined sobriquets: "Elvis the Pelvis," "Sir Swivel," "Wiggle Hips." Critics panned him, foreseeing a mercifully brief career, unaware that Elvis had picked up where Jimmy Dean had left off — symbol of juvenile rebellion. Like Dean, he had established a luster of being secretly "bad," with no apparent evidence to support this mysterious quality.

Jackie Gleason, at the peak of his video success, said flatly, "He can't last," little suspecting that he would be offering Elvis an enormous amount of money in 1962 for a guest appearance on his show — an appearance Presley refused to make because the fee was not up to his minimum.

The late Hedda Hopper loosed broadsides in her column that might have capsized a lesser man than Elvis. As Hollywood's one-woman Watch and Ward Society, Hopper cried out that Elvis was a menace to society and a threat to innocent children. Later Mrs. Hopper reappraised the singer: "The first night I tried dancing the Twist, I stopped suddenly and shrieked with laughter. I found myself doing what I'd condemned Elvis for doing. Now I am devoted to him. He's the best-mannered star in Hollywood, and he's improved as a performer and has a determination to become a fine actor. He was smart enough to simmer down that torrid act of his."

To moviemakers today, he is a freak. With little appeal to adult audiences, Elvis' pictures are without parallel as box-office guarantees. They are made for between $1,000,000 and $2,000,000, and gross upward of $6,000,000 — unfailingly.

Socially, Elvis might very well have remained a truck driver, for all the attention Hollywood's party givers pay him. By the same token, Elvis neither invites the "in" groups to his home nor joins the celebrity set in public places. Despite his aplomb and self-confidence among his own kind, he stands in awe of full-fledged stars, becoming more a fan than a peer of the Frank Sinatras and Marlon Brandos.

Elvis' appearances in public places are so rare that his presence in Hollywood frequently goes unnoticed. But his popularity is higher than that of any of the resident idols. Presley fan mail amounts to 15,000 letters every week, according to Tom Parker. It pours in to RCA-Victor, Twentieth Century-Fox, Paramount Studios, Hal Wallis, M-G-M, and the Mirisch Company, in addition to Graceland in Memphis and radio stations that play his records. His draw is equally strong abroad. In a recent poll sponsored by the London *Daily Express*, asking readers whom they would like most in the world to meet, Elvis ranked third, after Queen Elizabeth and Prince Philip, which may be quite a commentary on the intelligence of our times.

It is difficult to find anyone who has ever known Presley who will say anything demeaning about him. Such words as "humble," "polite," "well-mannered," "thoughtful" keep popping up.

But there is reason for this, too: Presley assiduously avoids contact with outsiders on all but the most superficial levels. People who might weigh and report his conversations and activities rarely have the opportunity to get close to him. Others — almost without exception those his own age or considerably younger — are allowed nearer; but they are either incapable of communicating his confidences or too afraid of losing his patronage to talk.

If there are any people in Hollywood who truly can claim to know the basic Presley, they are among the nine members of the Tennessee "gang," all or most of whom accompany him practically anywhere he goes, day or night, at work or at play. They are part of his life. At a sample day's shooting at the studio, each had his assigned duties, which began with Elvis' arrival with them in the two cars. Joe Esposito, minister of finance, ran over the day's possible expenses and petty cash. Gene Smith, Elvis' cousin and wardrobe master, hung up street clothes, checked on pressing. Other chores, including errands (called "gofor" duties), were shared by Billy Smith, Jim Kingsley, Red West, Rick Davis, and Sonny West. Outside, Allan Fortas, heavy-set and bull-strong, saw to the parking of automobiles, assisted by Ray ("The Chief") Sitton, second pilot of the Presley fleet of vehicles.

To a man, these quiet youths are dedicated to protecting Elvis from intrusion. It is a labor of love which carries with it Presley's friendship — a priceless status symbol — in addition to weekly salaries.

"They aren't employees," King Presley says, with cold resentment in his flat gray eyes. "These boys are my friends from down home. I've known them since we were kids together — all except Joe Esposito. He's an Army buddy who stayed with me when I got out."

This coterie that isolates Presley from Hollywood and the world is a conspiracy of silence. The boys refuse to discuss their leader's habits, attitudes, or character. They are wary and secretive, but physically well conditioned and attentive to all that goes on around them. They come in handy when a young tough throws a punch at Elvis in a crowd. The blow is stopped short of its mark, thereby freeing Elvis of embarrassing headlines the following day.

Because he spends almost half of every year in Hollywood, Presley's gang lives with him in the rented Bel-Air mansion. A couple (cook and butler) serve meals and do the cleaning.

The boy from Tennessee, actually a native of Tupelo, Mississippi, has become as adept at dodging matrimony as he has at escaping crowds of fans. He admits a hankering for marriage, but only in vague terms: "I want to get married and have children and all that. I'm still looking and shopping around. I almost got married when I was eighteen years old and fresh out of high school. My girlfriend still had one more year of school to finish. Then I started singing, and was away from town so much she got tired of waiting for me. Now she's married and has a couple of kids.

"Maybe I could fall in love and marry someday soon. But I'm not sure whether I've met the right girl or not. Trouble is, time passes too quickly in this business. I'm thirty-one, but I sure don't feel that old. I've been working so hard I haven't had time to get serious over a girl. When I marry, though, it'll be just for one time only. When a guy gets a wife, he's got to expect to simmer down and obey the rules. I'm all for it, but I think maybe I'll just wait a little while longer."

Elvis is so involved with his own pals that contacts with other members of the cast and crew of his pictures are necessarily restricted. Yet he is a favorite among the so-called "little people." He greets them by name, and depletes his store of small talk as the professional craftsmen and performers ask him for autographed photographs for their children.

The Presley entourage maintains its own version of North-South segregation in Hollywood. Elvis is not within musket distance of being a professional Southerner, but he and his boys share a suspicion of things Yankee that is not altogether unattractive. Their manners, speech, and behavior are graceful vestiges of the grand antebellum way of life, enough to draw solemn approval from the folks back home.

Mayor Henry Loeb, of Memphis, considers the singer a major Chamber of Commerce asset: "I don't call myself a close friend of Elvis', but I do know a lot about the boy, and all I hear is good. He is as generous and cooperative as a man can be. For instance, once word got to him that a young boy down in Florida was dying of cancer, and the only thing he wanted in life was to talk to Elvis Presley. Elvis called on him and sent him some albums. It meant all the world to that dying boy. Last year he put on a benefit show here and provided all the talent, music, and material to raise $50,000, and every cent of it went to charities in Memphis. He's a fine citizen, and I'm happy to say Elvis is just one swell guy."

Among the charities benefiting from Presley's show were the Crippled Children's Hospital, Convent of the Good Shepherd, Home for Incurables, Jewish Community Center, Junior League, St. Jude Hospital Foundation, and other organizations, representing many races and religions.

It is a fetish with Presley, as with Sinatra and some other stars, that his good deeds go unheralded. It is the modest thing to do, though often it is allowed to leak out.

Elvis' diet shocks Hollywood more than his pictures do, and provides endless discussion about his predilection for bananas and peanut-butter sandwiches, and cycles of preference for burned bacon, sauerkraut and gravy, or yoghurt and hamburgers.

Public response to Elvis and his fantastically lucrative contracts are principally the work of Colonel Tom Parker (the "Colonel" is honorary, bestowed in the vague past by a Tennessee official). Presley commonly credits Parker with his success: "I absolutely rely on the Colonel's judgment. He's a mighty fine businessman, and he's never let me do the wrong thing. He makes the deals, but my daddy and I take care of my own private financial affairs."

Elvis' father, Vernon Presley, headquartered in Memphis, is a former factory worker. He now devotes all his time to making investments and managing his son's vast fortune. Both are chary of stocks and bonds, preferring to keep the money in banks and in Tennessee real estate.

It requires an enormous amount of money for Elvis to maintain his standard of living. In addition to his asking price of $600,000 per picture, he receives 50 per cent of the profits. Other stars lay claim to equal or superior earnings, but they work far less frequently. In the past two years, Elvis has starred in six pictures. This is in addition to his ten-year RCA-Victor contract, which will pay him $3,000,000.

Presley fans are also able to buy many articles bearing his picture or name. They are handled by Henry Saperstein, president of Television Personalities, Inc., which now markets an even dozen Presley items, including charm bracelets, rings, wallets, stationery. Vice-president Harold Bell reveals that this Presleyana harvested $2,500,000 in retail sales during the past year. Elvis keeps approximately 2.5 per cent of that total.

A common question, asked and never answered, is: "What does he do with all his money?" Elvis isn't talking. But it was a simple matter to determine what happened to $50,000 just before last Christmas. Because he had promised Mayor Loeb that he would star in another benefit show for Memphis charities, Elvis was embarrassed when the press of work made it impossible for him to keep his word.

To make up for it, his father, in company with the Mayor's assistant, flew to Hollywood, where Elvis presented them with fifty checks, in the amount of $1,000 each, to be given to the same charities that had benefited from his show the previous year. The contributions came from his own pocket, and while a few small newspaper stories were printed, Elvis refused to make it a big promotion.

Because Elvis cannot enter restaurants or nightclubs without creating a major disturbance, he has turned to bringing selected strangers into his home. This accounts for his gang and the long get-togethers at his Bel-Air hide-out, a way of seeing new faces while controlling the adulation. For a man of his means, the soft drinks, pizzas, and hot dogs are little enough price to pay for this.

Elvis has worked himself into a corner where the more his fame grows, the less he is able to enjoy it. He likes watching football, for instance, but is afraid to go to the Los Angeles Coliseum for a Rams game. He's mobbed outside the gates, and once in his seat, he can't see the game for the fans who claw at him for attention, souvenirs, and autographs.

Doubtless, he is less mature than many thirty-one-year-olds, in or out of the limelight. But he is a millionaire, which sets him apart from most other men his age. He is also shrewd enough not to rock the boat.

His genius lies in communication with adolescents and segments of young people in their twenties. He uses their language — indeed invents part of it — plays the same practical jokes, and appears to be as self-conscious of puberty as they. In some respects, he reflects the Jimmy Dean syndrome. Young people realize that he is one of them and that he belongs to them. And this Elvis Presley knows instinctively.

He shares their suppressed hostility toward adults, their frustration in the face of authority. But he is a symbol of achievement, for he can buy his way free of grown-up supervision. He is a teen-age dream come true, a modern Peter Pan in Never-Never Land.

It is this conspiracy to confound age and maturity that welds Presley and his fans — his passport, if you will, to youth. An adult cannot put it into words, and if Elvis and his fans were able to do so, you may be sure they would keep it to themselves.

IN DEFENSE OF BOB DYLAN

Henrietta Yurchenco

In appearance the ultimate beatnik, Bobby Dylan is the high priest of the hybrid form of music he invented known as "folk rock." Dylan first bridged the gap between folk music and rock 'n' roll by adding a thumping big beat to verses of his "Subterranean Homesick Blues." Other folk-rock hits, including "Like a Rolling Stone," followed. Booed at first by folk-song purists, he nevertheless became a popular music idol. But Dylan did more than invent a new form of music. As a composer, his songs of social protest have sparked a revolution in popular music. The new hit songs are as apt to be about war, poverty, and civil rights as they are about teen-age love affairs. One of Dylan's most famous protest songs, "Blowin' in the Wind," has become the rallying song of the civil-rights movement.

It is the fate of every public figure, politician or theatrical personality, to live in a "goldfish bowl." According to their own prejudices, columnists, disc jockeys, magazine editors, aficionados, and the public at large all condemn and praise, spread rumors and idle gossip, and offer gratuitous and irrelevant predictions. "He's a bum," says one. "He's the White Hope," says the other. And there is nothing to be done about it! 'Tis the nature of the beast.

A recent target for this sort of public scrutiny is young Bob Dylan from Minnesota. Dylan made a stir the first time he walked into a Greenwich Village coffee house and offered a song for his supper, and has been making one ever since. Today he is a star entertainer, adored by young people throughout the country, imitated by a host of pop singers and instrumentalists. His record sales are astronomical, his appearances in universities and concert halls always S.R.O.

Everything Dylan does causes controversy. Even his clothes start tongues wagging. When Bob appeared for the first time, he looked like all the other folk singers, wearing blue jeans and a railroad worker's cap (he told me it was for taking up collections). Today he wears bright, expensive shirts and fancy boots. His mop of long curly hair hangs down almost to his shoulders.

His several TV appearances on the Steve Allen and Les Crane shows were nothing short of disastrous. Dylan refused to play the game according to the rules: he balked at talk and vapid TV repartee — but he did sing! Why in the world anyone asks him to do what he patently can't or won't do, and why he accepts engagements of this kind, is utterly baffling. Certainly money is not the whole explanation. Several years ago, just at the beginning of his meteoric rise to fame, Dylan came down to WNYC for an interview (unpaid) on my program, "Adventures in Folk Music." The "interview" was a fiasco; in front of the mike, conversation bogged down hopelessly. Finally, engineer and production personnel said good-bye and disappeared. Then, and only then, did Dylan talk. In response to a single question, he spoke for two hours

— eloquently, brilliantly, and provocatively — but not for taping!

In our age of overexposure, it is apparently not enough to excel in one's field; one must be articulate about it and about oneself, and be available and responsive to public and critical demand and instruction. I suspect that even our astronauts are selected not only for scientific qualifications and physical endurance, but also, to some degree, for their effectiveness before a microphone.

The controversy over Bob Dylan as a poet extends beyond the minor points mentioned above. Literary academicians also have their say. The publication *Books* conducted a poll of professors, critics, and poets which brought the following responses. Said Howard Nemerov: "Mr. Dylan is not known to me. Regrets." An English professor at the University of Vermont commented: "Anyone who calls Bob Dylan 'the greatest poet in the United States today' has rocks in his head . . . Dylan is for the birds — and the bird-brained." . . . "His poetry sounds like a very self-conscious imitation of Kerouac, and for an English teacher this is pretty feeble praise. My students . . . have lost respect for Dylan, for they think he is after publicity and the nearest buck." John Ciardi wrote: "My nephew (a drummer) would agree that Bob Dylan is a poet, but like all Bob Dylan fans I have met, he knows nothing about poetry. Neither does Bob Dylan." A few, like John Clellan Holmes, went to his defense: "He has the authentic mark of the bard on him, and

Bob Dylan

I think it's safe to say that no one, years hence, will
be able to understand just what it was like to live in
this time without attending to what this astonishingly
gifted young man has already achieved." All shades
of opinion were represented — from blind hostility to
unqualified praise, and also the indifference of an older
generation forgetful of its own rebellious youth.

If Bob Dylan has done nothing else, he is responsible for the present widespread interest in poetry. He
has taken it away from the academicians, off the dusty
library shelves, and put it where it can be heard by
countless thousands of young people. In our unpoetic
age, where an audience of a few hundred people
at a poetry reading is unusual, Dylan's feat is quite
remarkable.

From the start, Dylan's poetry was characterized not
only by the acuteness and individuality of his vision,
but by his gift for words and imagery. His poetic tools
have been sharpened, particularly in his recent album
Highway 61 Revisited. Virtuosity for its own sake,
which sometimes needlessly halted the poetic flow, is
now not so pronounced. Though still stunning and
often startling, his images are more related to the cen-
tral theme; therefore his construction is more disci-
plined, less erratic.

Dylan may be a popular poet, but he is not a simple-
ton, as some of his critics imply. He is very well read
— and a poet of his time. Stanley Kunitz, quoted in
Thomas Meehan's *New York Times* article, says:
". . . and popular art is the foundation on which fine
art rests. Thus, the higher the level of taste there is
in the popular arts, the more promising is the hope

for the evolution of great fine art." But even more to the point is Kunitz' statement ". . . There is no reason why popular art and a more selective, esoteric art can't cheerfully coexist."

The folk-music community has been shaken to its very roots ever since Dylan appeared at the Newport Folk Festival in the summer of 1965 with Paul Butterfield's Blue Band. Writing in *Sing Out*, the nation's leading folk-music magazine, Paul Nelson stated that Newport 1965 split apart the two biggest names in folk music: Pete Seeger (who had the backing of the crowd) and Bob Dylan (who was booed off the stage). He writes: "They [the audience] might have believed they were choosing humanity over a reckless me-for-me attitude, but they weren't. They were choosing suffocation over invention and adventure, backwards over forwards, a dead hand instead of a live one." For Nelson also it seems only a matter of Seeger versus Dylan — whether to accept Pete's quest for a better, more brotherly world, or Bob's, "where things aren't often pretty, where there isn't often hope, where man isn't always noble, but where, most importantly, there exists a reality that coincides with that of this planet. Was it to be marshmallows and cotton candy or meat and potatoes?" The choice (continues Mr. Nelson) is between "A nice guy who has subjugated and weakened his art through his constant insistence on a world that never was and never can be, or an angry, passionate poet who demands his art to be all, who demands not to be owned, not to be restricted. . . ."

This oversimplification does gross injustice to Seeger, Dylan, and the audience. It underestimates the great

range of Seeger's seasoned understanding and over-
estimates the profundity of young Dylan's insights. It
reflects a recurrent (and regrettable) need of both
aficionados and critics, the need for "variety" in their
diet of hero worship, which partly explains why they
periodically provide their heroes with a pedestal and
just as regularly yank it from under them — a pedestal
their heroes never asked for in the first place, by the
way. Why in the name of good folk music should anyone have to "choose between two such authentic (and
different) artists as Seeger and Dylan? Cannot we
"choose" *both*?

Mr. Nelson makes more sense on the subject of the
artist's freedom to write when and how he pleases.
Even before Newport, Dylan's free-wheeling wander-
ing from the topical-song field had kicked up a storm
in folk-song circles. What a blow it was to have the
most gifted songwriter since Guthrie not only "desert"
the ranks, but disassociate himself from the "movement" entirely! The fact that Bob has never pretended
to be solely a protest songwriter has not stopped his
critics from either condemning him or preaching the
path of righteousness to him, or warning him of the
dire pitfalls of commercial success.

In one of my talks with Bob at the outset of his
career, he described the early months in New York:
"I wrote wherever I happened to be. Sometimes I'd
spend a whole day sitting at a corner table in a coffee
house just writing whatever came into my head . . .
just anything. I'd look at people for hours, and I'd
make up things about them; or I'd think, what kind
of song would they like to hear, and I'd make one up."

Hardly the words of a young writer concerned only with the hot issues of the outer world.

If it were only a question of entertainment criteria, if Dylan were only another Rudy Vallee, Frank Sinatra, Eddie Fisher, or Bing Crosby (all great performers in the popular field), we would have nothing to talk about. But Dylan is different from them all; he is a creator, and he has his literary finger on the pulse of the perplexing problems that beset young people today. His subjects, whether they concern (as they did until recently) political and social issues, or whether they reflect inner problems (his current preoccupation), are all germane to our times and his life.

Whether Dylan is a great poet, history will have to decide, but he is unquestionably our most popular. He has given poetry a significance and stature which it has never had in American life. Furthermore, he is a bard — a singing poet in an ancient but thoroughly neglected tradition.

European, Near and Far Eastern, and African epic poets have for thousands of years sung their national chronicles. Today, epic poetry (sung poetry) is an important factor in the national culture and has passed into the literary traditions of other lands. Not even such fine poets as Walt Whitman and Robert Frost — among our greatest — were truly popular poets; they were known mainly to intellectuals. This is not, of course, to imply that all popular poets are great, nor that the stature of the others is diminished.

In his latest albums, *Bringing It All Back Home* and *Highway 61 Revisited*, Dylan sings of the chaos and the absurdities of our changing world, the lack of understanding between adults and the young. He ridicules the dullness, the inadequacies and pointlessness of academic life. He chides those of his own generation who would settle for a comfortable, protected world; who let others make decisions for them; who prefer status and security to adventure in life. Of the fearful he says, "There're some people terrified of the bomb, but there are other people terrified to be seen carrying a modern screen magazine." He speaks out frankly about love and sex. His poetry reflects a positive attitude; it seems to urge: live as fully and purposefully as possible, intellectually and emotionally. Obviously Dylan is still a protest writer — what else could he be called?

The subjects of Dylan's songs, the substance of his thoughts, are neither startling nor new. The "sexual revolution" which began after World War I is still growing; this present generation has already reaped some advantage from it. (At least teen-agers can talk about it at the dinner table.) As for the academic world, when has it not been under fire from hot youth? What makes Dylan's poetic themes relevant today — in short, what is "new" — is today's frame of reference. Never before has mankind been threatened, as we are today, with *total destruction*; that is why attitudes toward pleasure for its own sake, the absurdity of life, the desire to escape (or to stand fast and accomplish), are all proper grist for his poetic mill. Because he is a poet, and young, Dylan is frequently impatient, disgusted, intolerant. But one thing is certain: for the young people, whose passionate challenge to the world and its values has not yet been "tempered" by the wear-and-tear of the years or by the weary cynicism that too often passes for wisdom, and who seem to sense, even when they cannot always critically evaluate, the meaning of his poetry, Bob Dylan is the most popular, the most powerful figure of our time.

The music in Dylan's first albums was in the mainstream of American folk music of the early 1960's. The sources of his musical settings were blues, southern Appalachian country music, traditional ballads, Woody Guthrie, and early Elvis Presley (before his snakehipping era). Accompanying himself on guitar and harmonica, Bob emulated country rather than city style. His singing was crude, direct, unembellished, and very appropriate to his material. Then came the switch to rock 'n' roll, or folk rock, as the combination of folk tune and electrified instruments is called. On the basis of this development (hardly new, for Dylan had been playing popular piano for a long time), he has been roundly condemned by folk-music fans.

Duane Eddy, the well-known rock-'n'-roll man, has recently recorded Dylan's tunes in instrumental arrangements, and it is quite surprising how good they really are. While it is true that the engineering on *Highway 61 Revisited*, all folk rock, makes it almost impossible to hear the words over the metallic clang of the instrumental backing, it should not obscure the fact that the album has some great tunes. Some of it is very exciting, but an entire LP of clang, clang, heard at top volume (a necessary condition for listening), is exhausting. What I find unpardonable is the lack of song texts. It has long been the practice of many recording companies to include the words on the album jacket. Why not on Dylan's, where the words are absolutely necessary? Most listeners I know rehear each song a dozen times, writing the words as best they can. A book of lyrics of *Highway 61 Revisited* is now in the music stores, so if you want to get the maximum benefit, another investment — a book — is necessary.

Time will tell whether Dylan is a flash in the pan or of lasting importance. I hope Bob will decide for himself what his next move will be, without the "advice" of either his doting admirers or his critics. He has a basic honesty which should see him through. When his first album appeared, my review in *The American Record Guide* was unfavorable. When we met for the first time, Bob looked me squarely in the eye and said, "I read your review . . . ." "I'm sorry," I said, "I didn't like that record!" "Oh, that's all right," he said, smiling shyly, "it *was* terrible, and you were the only one who said so. Thanks!"

His present disassociation from the issues of war, integration, and nuclear destruction may only be temporary. Part of his irritation may undoubtedly be attributed to the pontifical and patronizing hounding of the people in the topical-song field. But nothing is forever. Dylan has shown his ability to express contemporary life on many levels, all of them valid and pertinent to our time. If he chooses to ignore the political scene today, that is his privilege; but no one can accuse him of hiding in an ivory tower. No one denies the urgency of such issues as war and peace, integration, and the war on poverty, but this hardly justifies anyone's settings himself up as censor. Will success corrupt him? That remains to be seen. For the present, in this time of dreary conformity and intellectual cowardice in the face of a world gone mad, Dylan's words and music are fresh and alive, and deserve to be heard.

THE FIRST TYCOON OF TEEN
Tom Wolfe

At seventeen he wrote his first rock-'n'-roll hit, a song called "To Know Him Is to Love Him." The title came from an inscription on his father's tombstone. At nineteen he was a recording company executive, and before long had his own company. He made his first million by the time he was twenty-one. Today, at twenty-four, Phil Spector is called the Genius of Teen. Since October, 1962, he has produced twenty-one records that have sold more than 13,000,000 copies. But Spector doesn't laugh all the way to the bank. An intense young man, he broods about "cigar-smoking sharpies" (record distributors), people who twit him about his long hair, and people who put down rock 'n' roll, accusing him of poisoning American culture and rotting the minds of youth.

Phil Spector is sitting in a little cream room in his office suite at 440 East 62nd Street with his back to a window that is practically on top of the East Side Drive. Twenty-four years old, he has a complex of corporations known as Phil Spector Productions. One of them is Mother Bertha Productions, named after his mother, Bertha. She works for his office in Los Angeles, but only because she wants to. The main organization is Philles Records. Spector has produced twenty-one "single" Philles records since October, 1962, and sold more than 13,000,000 copies. All rock 'n' roll. His big hit, "Walking in the Rain," by the Ronettes, went as high Number 20 on the cashbox chart and sold more than 250,000 copies. His latest record, "You've Lost That Lovin' Feelin'," by the Righteous Brothers, rose from the twenties to Number 37 with a "bullet" beside it, meaning "going up fast." He has produced seven albums. The first teen-age tycoon! He is leaning back in the chair. He has on a suede jerkin, Italian pants, a pair of pointy British boots with Cuban heels. His hair hangs down to his shoulders in back. The beard is shaved off, however.

Danny Davis, his promotion man, is talking on the phone in the inner office. A fellow sits across from Spector with his legs crossed and a huge chocolate-brown Borsalino hat over his bent knee, as if he were just trying it on. He says, "Phil, why do you do —"

"I'm moving the whole thing to California," says Phil Spector. "I can't stand flying any more."

"— why do you do these things?"

Spector — without his beard, Spector has a small chin, a small head; his face looks at first like all those little kids with bad hair and reedy voices from the Bronx, where he was born. But — an *ordinary* Phil Spector? Phil Spector has the only pure American voice. He was brought up not in the Bronx, but in California. His voice meanders, quietly, shaking, through his doldrum fury out to somewhere beyond cynical, beyond cool, beyond teen-age world-weary. It is thin, broken, and soft. He is only twenty-three years old, the first millionaire businessman to rise up out of the teen-age netherworld, king of the rock-'n'-roll record producers.

Spector jumps out of the chair. "Wait a minute," he says. "Just a minute. They're making deals in here."

Spector walks into the inner office gingerly, like a cowboy, because of the way the English boots lift him up off the floor. He is slight, five feet seven, 130 pounds. His hair shakes faintly behind. It is a big room, like a living room, all beige except for eight gold-plated rock-'n'-roll records on the wall — some of Phil Spector's "goldies," 1,000,000 sales each. "He's a Rebel," by the Crystals. "Zip-a-dee-doo-dah," by Bob B. Soxx and the Blue Jeans. "Be My Baby," by the Ronettes. "Da Do Ron Ron," "Then He Kissed Me," "Uptown," "He's Sure the Boy I Love," all by the Crystals. "Wait Till My Baby Gets Home," by Darlene Love. And beige walls, beige telephones all over the place, a beige upright piano, beige paintings, beige tables, with Danny Davis crowding over a beige desk, talking on the telephone.

"Sure, Sal," says Danny, "I'll ask Phil. Maybe we can work something out on that."

Spector starts motioning thumbs down.

"Just a minute, Sal." Danny puts his hand over the mouthpiece and says, "We *need* this guy, Phil. He's the biggest distributor out there. He wants the 1,000 guarantee."

Phil's hands go up as if he were lifting a slaughtered lamb up on top of an icebox. "I don't care. I'm not interested in the money, I've got millions, I don't care who needs this animal. I'm interested in selling records, O.K.? Why should I give him a guarantee? He orders the records, I guarantee I'll buy 1,000 back from him if he can't sell them; he sells them, then after the record dies he buys up 500 cut-rate from somebody, sends them back, and cries for his money. Why should we have to be eating his singles later?"

Danny takes his hand away and says into the mouthpiece: "Look, Sal, there's one thing I forgot. Phil says this record he can't give the guarantee. But you don't have anything to worry about . . . I know what I said, but Phil says . . . look, Sal, don't worry, 'Walking in the Rain,' this is a tremendous record — tremendous, a very big record . . . What? . . . I'm not reading off a paper, Sal . . . Wait a minute, Sal —"

"Who needs these animals?" Spector tells Danny.

"Look, Sal," Danny says, "this man never made a bad record in his life. You tell me one. Nothing but hits."

"Tell him I'm not in," says Spector.

"Sal —"

"Who needs these animals!" says Spector, so loud this time that Danny cups his hand around the receiver and puts his mouth down close.

"Nothing, Sal," says Danny, "that was somebody came in."

"Joan," says Phil, and a girl, Joan Berg, comes in out of another room. "Will you turn the lights off?" he says.

She turns the lights off, and now in the middle of the day the offices of Philles Records and Mother Bertha Productions are all dark except for the light from Danny Davis' lamp. Danny crowds into the pool of light, hunched over the phone, talking to Sal.

Phil puts his fingers between his eyes and wraps his eyebrows around them.

"Phil, it's dark in here," says the fellow with the large hat. "Why do you do these things?"

"I'm paying a doctor $600 a week to find out," says Phil, without looking up.

He sits there in the dark, his fingers buried between his eyes. Just over his head one can make out a painting. The painting is kind of came-with-the-frame surrealist. It shows a single musical note, a half note, suspended over what looks like the desert outside Las Vegas. Danny has to sit there huddled in his own pool of light talking to this "animal" on the telephone.

"This is primitive country," says Phil Spector. "I was at Shepheard's, the discothèque, and these guys start saying these things. It's unbelievable. These people are animals."

"What kind of thing, Phil?"

"I don't know. They look at, you know, my hair. My wife and I are dancing, and — I mean it's unbelievable — I feel somebody yanking on my hair in the back. I turn around, and here's this guy, a grown man, and he is saying these unbelievable things to me. So I tell him, like this, "I'm going to tell you this one time, that's all: don't ever try that again." And the guy it's unbelievable — he shoves me with the heel of his hand and I go sprawling back into a table —"

Spector pauses.

"— I mean, I've studied karate for years. I could literally kill a guy like that. You know? Size means nothing. A couple of these —" he cocks his elbow in the gloom and brings up the flat of his forearm — "but what am I going to do, start a fight every time

Phil Spector

I go out? Why should I even have to listen to anything from these animals? I find this country very
condemning. I don't have this kind of trouble in
Europe. The people of America are just not born with
culture."

Not born with culture! If only David Susskind and
William B. Williams could hear that. Susskind invited
Phil Spector to the "Open End" television program
one evening to talk about the record business. Suddenly Susskind and William B., station WNEW's old-
nostalgia disc jockey, were condemning Spector as one
kind of sharpie poisoning American culture, rotting
the minds of youth, and so forth. That was how it all
hit Spector. It was as if he were some kind of old
short-armed fatty in the Brill Building, the music center on Broadway, with a spread-collar shirt and a bald
olive skull with strands of black hair pulled up over
it from above one ear. There was something very ironic
about that. Spector is the one record producer who
wouldn't go near Broadway. His setup is practically
out in the East River, up by the Rockefeller Institute.

Susskind and Williams kept throwing Spector's songs
at him — "He's a Rebel," "Da Do Ron Ron," "Be My
Baby," "Fine Fine Boy," "Breakin' Up" — as if he
were astutely conning millions of the cretins out there
with this stuff. Spector didn't know exactly what to
tell them. He *likes* the music he produces. He writes
it himself. He is something new: the first teen-age
millionaire, the first boy to become a millionaire within
America's teen-age netherworld. It was never a simple
question of his taking a look at the rock-'n'-roll universe from the outside and exploiting it. He stayed
within it himself. He *liked* the music.

Spector, while still in his teens, seemed to compre-
hend the prole vitality of rock 'n' roll that has made
it the kind of darling holy beast of intellectuals in the
United States, England, and France. Intellectuals, generally, no longer take jazz seriously. Monk, Mingus,
Ferguson — it has all been left to little executive train-
ees with their first apartment and a mahogany African
mask from the free-port shop in Haiti and a hi-fi. But
rock 'n' roll! Poor old arteriosclerotic lawyers with
pocky layers of fat over their ribs are out there right
now twisting clumsily to rock 'n' roll. Their wives
wear stretch pants to the seafood shop. A style of life!

There have been teen-agers who have made a million dollars before, but invariably they are entertain-
ers; they are steered by older people, such as the good
Colonel Tom Parker who steers Elvis Presley. But Phil
Spector is the bona fide genius of teen. Every baroque
period has a flowering genius who rises up as the
most glorious expression of its style of life — in latter-
day Rome, the Emperor Commodus; in Renaissance
Italy, Benvenuto Cellini; in late Augustan England,
the Earl of Chesterfield; in the sad, volatile Victorian
age, Dante Gabriel Rossetti; in late-fancy, neo-Greek
federal America, Thomas Jefferson; and in teen America, Phil Spector.

In point of fact, he had turned twenty-one when he
made his first clear million. But it was as a teen-ager,
working within the teen-age milieu, starting at the age
of seventeen, that Phil Spector developed into a great
American businessman, the greatest of the independent
rock-'n'-roll record producers. Spector's mother, Bertha,
took him from the Bronx to California when he was
nine. California! Teen heaven! By the time he was six-

teen he was playing jazz guitar with some group. Then
he got interested in rock 'n' roll, which he does not
call "rock 'n' roll" but "pop blues." That is because —
well, that's a complicated subject. Anyway, Phil Spector
likes this music. He genuinely likes it. He is not a short-
armed fatty hustling nutball fads.

"I get a little angry when people say it's bad music,"
Spector tells the man with the brown hat. "This music
has a spontaneity that doesn't exist in any other kind
of music, and it's what is here now. It's unfair to
classify it as rock 'n' roll and condemn it. It has
limited chord changes, and people are always saying
the words are banal and why doesn't anybody write
lyrics like Cole Porter any more, but we don't have
any Presidents like Lincoln any more, either. You
know? Actually, it's more like the blues. It's pop blues.
I feel it's very American. It's very *today*. It's what
people respond to today. It's not just the kids. I hear
cab drivers, everybody, listening to it."

And Susskind sits there on his show reading one of
Spector's songs out loud — no music, just reading the
words, from the "Top Sixty" or whatever it is — "Fine
Fine Boy," to show how banal rock 'n' roll is. The
song just keeps repeating "He's a fine fine boy." So
Spector starts drumming on the big coffee table there
with the flat of his hands in time to Susskind's voice
and says, "What you're missing is the beat." Blam
blam.

Everybody is getting a little sore, with Susskind
reading these simple lyrics and Spector blamming away
on the coffee table. Finally Spector starts asking Williams how may times he plays Verdi on his show?
— Monteverdi? — D. Scarlatti? — A. Scarletti? "That's

good music, why don't you play that? You keep saying you play only good music. I don't hear you playing that." Williams doesn't know what to say. Spector tells Susskind he didn't come on the show to listen to somebody tell him he was corrupting the youth of America — he could be home making money. Susskind: "Well, ah, all right, Phil." Everybody is testy.

Making money. Yes! At the age of seventeen Spector wrote a rock-'n'-roll song called "To Know Him Is to Love Him." He took the title off his father's tombstone. That was what his mother had had engraved on his father's tombstone out in Beth David Cemetery in Elmont, Long Island. He doesn't say much about his father, just that he was "average lower middle class." Spector wrote the song, sang it, and played the guitar in the recording with a group called the Teddy Bears. He made $20,000 on that record, but somebody ran off with $17,000 of it, and . . . well, no use going into that. Then he was going to UCLA, but he couldn't afford it and became a court reporter — one of the people who sit at the shorthand machine taking down testimony. He decided to come to New York and get a job as interpreter at the U.N. His mother had taught him French. But he got to New York, and the night before the interview he fell in with some musicians and never got there. Instead he wrote another hit that year, "Spanish Harlem." And then — only nineteen — he became head of A. & R., Artists and Repertoire, for Atlantic Records. By 1961 he was a free-lance producer, producing records for the companies, working with Connie Francis, Elvis Presley, Ray Peterson, the Paris Sisters.

All this time Spector would write a song and run

all phases of making records, get the artists, direct the
recording sessions — everything. Spector would work
with these kids who make these records because he was
a kid himself, in one sense. God knows what the music-
business biggies thought of Phil Spector — he already
wore his hair like Salvador Dali did at that age, or
like an old mezzotint of Mozart or something. And
he was somehow *one of them* — the natives, the kids
who sang and responded to this . . . music. Phil
Spector could get in one of those studios with the
heron microphones, a representative of the adult world
that makes money from records, and it became all one
thing: the kids comprehended him.

Spector had an ideal: Archie Bleyer. Bleyer was a
band leader who founded a record company, Cadence
Records. Spector formed a partnership with two other
people in 1961, then bought them out and went on
his own as Philles Records in October of 1962. His
first big hit was "He's a Rebel," by the Crystals. Spector
had a system. The big record companies put out records
like buckshot — ten, maybe fifteen rock-'n'-roll records
a month — and if one of them catches on, they can
make money. Spector's system is to put them out one
at a time, and pour everything into each one. Spector
does the whole thing. He writes the words and the
music, scouts and signs up the talent. He takes them
out to a recording studio in Los Angeles and runs the
recording session himself. He puts them through hours
and days of recording to get the two or three minutes
he wants. Two or three minutes out of the whole strug-
gle. He handles the control dials like an electronic
maestro, tuning various instruments or sounds up,
down, out, every which way, using things like two

pianos, a harpsichord, and three guitars on one record; then rerecording the whole thing with esoteric dubbing and overdubbing effects — reinforcing instruments or voices — coming out with what is known through the industry as "the Spector sound." The only thing he doesn't keep control of is the actual manufacture, the pressing of the records and the distribution.

The only people around to give him any trouble all this time are the distributors, cigar-chewing fatties, and . . . well, to be honest, there is a lot that gives Phil Spector trouble, and it's not so much any kind of or any group of people as much as his status. A teen-age tycoon! He is betwixt and between. He identifies with the teen-age netherworld, he defends it, but he is already too mature for it. As a millionaire, a business genius, living in a penthouse twenty-two stories up over the East River, with his wife, Annette, who is twenty, a student at Hunter College, and with a four-room suite downstairs on the ground floor as his office, and a limousine, and a chauffeur, and a bodyguard, and a staff — Danny and Joan Berg and everybody — and a doorman who directs people to Mr. Spector's office . . . well, that makes Phil Spector one of *them*, the universe of arteriosclerotic, hypocritical, cigar-chewing, hopeless, larded adults, infracted vultures one meets in the music business. And so here in the dark is a twenty-four-year old man with a Shelley visage, a suede shirt, a kind of page-boy bob and winkle-picker boots — the symbol of the teen world — sitting in the dark in this great beige office — the symbol of the tycoon world — in the middle of the day, in the dark, tamping his frontal lobes with his fingers in the gloom.

One of the beige phones rings and Danny answers. Then he presses the "hold" button and tells Phil Spector, "It's the Rolling Stones. They just got in."

Spector comes alive with that. He gets up on his ginger toes and goes to the telephone. He is lively, and he spins on the balls of his feet a little as he stands by the phone.

"Hello, Andrew," he says. He is talking with Andrew Oldham, the manager of the Rolling Stones. And then he puts on a Cockney accent, "Are you all in?" he says.

The Rolling Stones — all right. The Rolling Stones, English group, and Andrew Oldham, are like him. They grew up in the teen-age netherworld and made it, and they all want to have it all too, the kids' style of life and the adult's — money — and not cop out on one side or the other, larded and arteriosclerotic. Phil Spector's British trip! That was where suddenly he had it all.

Phil Spector is here! The British had the ability to look at all sorts of rebel baddies and alienated thin young fellows and say coo and absorb them like a great soggy, lukewarm, mother's poultice. The Beatles, Beatlemania, rock 'n' roll — suddenly it is all absorbed into the center of things as if it could have been there all along if it only asked. Phil Spector arrives at London Airport and, Santa Barranza, there are photographers all over the place, for him, Phil Spector, and the next morning he is all over the center fold of the *London Daily Mirror*, the biggest newspaper in the Western World, 5,000,000 circulation: "The 23-year-old American rock-'n'-roll magnate." He is in the magazines as the "U. S. Recording Tycoon." Invitations go out to come to the receptions to meet "America's outstanding hit maker, Phil Spector." And then he lands back at Idlewild and waiting are, yes, the same bunch of cheese-breath cabbies, and he takes a cab on back to 440 East 62nd Street and goes into his beige world — the phones are ringing and it is all the same, the same. . . .

"Cigar-smoking sharpies," says Phil Spector. He is in a livelier mood after the talk with Andrew Oldham. "They're a bunch of cigar-smoking sharpies in record distribution. They've all been in the business for years, and they resent you if you're young. That's one reason so many kids go broke in this business. They're always starting new record companies — or they used to, the business is very soft right now. They start a company and pour all their money into a record, and it can be successful and they're still broke, because these characters don't even pay you until you've had three or four hit records in a row. They order the records and sell them and don't pay you. They don't pay you because they know they don't have to. You start yelling for the money and they tell you, "What-ya mean, I have all these records coming back from the retailers, and what about my right to return records and blah-blah! What are you going to do? Sue twenty guys in twenty different courts in the United States?

"They look at everything as a product. They don't care about the work and sweat you put into a record. They respect me now because I keep turning out hits, and after that they become sort of honest . . . in their own decayed way."

Where does a man find friends, comrades, anything, in a world like that? They resent his youth. They resent his success. But it is no better with the kids.

He is so much more mature and more . . . eminent
. . . they all want to form "the father thing" with
him. Or else they want to fawn over him, cozen him,
cajole, fall down before him, whistle, shout, stomp,
bang him on the head — anything to get his attention
and get "the break," just one chance. Or one more
chance. Spector can't go near the Brill Building, the
center of the music business, because the place is crawl-
ing with kids with winkle-picker shoes cracking in
the folds who made one hit record five years ago and
still can't realize that they are now, forever, in oblivion.
They crawl all over the place, the way the small-time
balding fatty promoters and managers used to in the
days when A. J. Liebling wrote about the place as the
Jollity Building.

Phil Spector steps onto an elevator in the Brill
Building. The elevator is packed, and suddenly he feels
this arm hooking through his in the most hideously
cozy way and a mouth is closing in on his ear and
saying, "Phil, baby, wait'll you hear this one: 'Ooh-
oom-bah-ay,'" and Phil Spector is imprisoned there
with the elevator inching up, "'vah ump nooby poon
fan ooh-ooh ayub bah-ay' — you dig that, Phil? You
dig that, don't you, Phil? Phil, babes!" He walks down
the hall and kids sneak up behind him and slip songs,
music, lyrics into his coat pocket. He finds the stuff
in there, all this ratty paper, when he gets home. Or
he is leaving the Brill Building and he feels a great
whack on the back of his head and wheels around,
and there are four kids in the singing stance, their
heads angled in together, saying, "Just one bar, Phil:
'Say wohna love boo-uh-ay-yay-bubby,'" while the guy
on the end sings bass with his chin mashed into a

pulpy squash down over his collarbone ". . . 'beh-ungggh, beh-ungggh.' "

Status! What is his status? He produces rock 'n' roll, and therefore he is not a serious person and he won't join the Young Presidents or whatever kind of organization jaycee geniuses would join for their own good.

"Phil," says the man with the hat, "why don't you hire a press agent, a P.R. man?"

Phil is tamping his frontal lobes in the gloom. Danny Davis is hunched up in the little pool of light on his desk. Danny is doing his level best for Phil.

"Jack? Danny Davis . . . Yeah . . . No, I'm with Phil Spector now . . . Right! It's the best move I ever made. You know Phil . . . I'm in the best shape of my career . . . Jack, I just want to tell you we've got —"

"A press agent?" Phil says to the man in the hat. "In the first place, I couldn't stand to hear what he'd say about me."

"— got two tremendous records going, Jack, 'Walk-in the Rain,' the Ronettes, and —"

"In the second place," Phil says, "there's no way my image can be bought."

"— and 'You've Lost That Lovin' Feelin'' by the Righteous Brothers," says Danny. ". . . Right, Jack. . . . I appreciate that, Jack . . ."

"The only thing I could do — you know what I'd like to do? I'd like to do a recording session in the office of *Life* or *Esquire* or *Time*, and then they could see it. That's the only chance I've got. Because I'm dealing in rock 'n' roll, it's like I'm not a bona fide human being."

". . . Absolutely! . . . If there's anything we can

do for you on this end, Jack, let us know. O.K.?
Great, Jack . . ."

"And I even have trouble with people who should
never say *any*thing. I go over to Gristede's to get a
quart of milk or something, and the women at the
cash register has to start in. So I tell her, 'There's a
war in Viet Nam, they've fired Khrushchev, the Repub-
lican party is falling to pieces, the Ku Klux Klan is
running around loose, and you're worrying about my
hair!' "

America's first teen-age tycoon — a business genius,
a musical genius — and it is as if he were still on the
corner of Hoffman Street in the Bronx when the big
kids come by in hideous fraternity, the way these people act. What is he now? Who is he in this weird
country? Danny talks in the phone in the little pool
of light; Joan is typing up whatever it is; Phil is
tamping his frontal lobes.

WHAT DO THEY GET FROM ROCK 'N' ROLL?

Jeremy Larner

*How does one account for the phenomenal popularity of rock
'n' roll among teen-agers? There is, says author Jeremy Larner,
a general need for rock 'n' roll — a need rooted in strong feelings,
a need fulfilled by the one standard ingredient of all rock 'n' roll:
its steady, heavy, simple beat, which submerges earthly worries
in a tide of rising exaltation. Moreover, through rock 'n' roll
teen-agers learn to handle their aggressions and discontents.
It is a relatively harmless outlet for the antisocial feelings brought
on by their frustrations. Lastly, rock 'n' roll provides a special
product by which teen-agers can identify themselves. Others may
listen to rock 'n' roll, but it belongs peculiarly to the teen-agers.*

On April 23, 1956, when the style of music known
as rock 'n' roll had already established its present-day
popularity, 3,500 citizens of Birmingham, Alabama,
formed a lily-white audience for Negro singer Nat
King Cole, who almost never sang in the rock idiom.
To the dismay of his Birmingham admirers, Cole was
interrupted by a delegation of hoods from the White
Citizens Council, who jumped on stage and started to
beat him. When questioned by reporters, a spokesman
for the W.C.C. said that jazz in general was part of

the N.A.A.C.P.'s "plot to mongrelize America. Rock 'n' roll," he said, "is the basic, heavy-beat music of the Negroes. It appeals to the base in man, brings out animalism and vulgarity."

Though the White Citizen had his own special ax to grind, his was not the only American civic group to express concern about the raucous new music which began in 1954 to saturate the airwaves and jukeboxes. By 1956 many church and community organizations had gone so far as to insist that rock 'n' roll be outlawed, for rock-'n'-roll concerts had been followed by teen-age riots in Hartford, Washington, Minneapolis, Boston, Atlanta, and Oakland, as well as in Birmingham. Various highbrows and middlebrows have complained ever since that rock 'n' roll is the result of a vicious business conspiracy intent on mass-producing the cheapest, simplest music and pushing it like dope to the vulnerable masses. Yet despite the value judgments which rock 'n' roll constantly inspires, no one has seriously attempted to tell us what rock 'n' roll is or why it remains so popular.

The technical ingredients of rock 'n' roll are simple. The traditional thirty-two-bar pop-song structure has been mostly dispensed with; instead, the musicians simply repeat eight-bar measures. Harmonically, rock 'n' roll also relies on repetition: standard triads are lined up in repeating triplets behind a steady four-beat rhythm. The most common instrument is the home-learned guitar played in one key only. The country or Negro inflections are essential no matter where a singer comes from, so much so that even the Beatles — who flowered, as everyone knows, in Liverpool — sing in accents of rural Tennessee.

In the history of jazz, there is a long tradition of white musicians smoothing out and popularizing what Negro performers begin. In prewar days, it was the white swing bands that America danced to, although most of their material had been originated by Negro bands still largely confined to the ghettos. Perhaps it was only natural that as World War II was ending, a new generation of disillusioned urban Negro musicians introduced a style of jazz "that the whites can't copy." Behop, as the new music later came to be called, relied on the jarring harmonies of flatted fifths and polytonal chords, punctuated by nervous, aggressive rhythms — with the result that the teen-age set found this new jazz nearly impossible to dance to. The big dance bands had broken up during the war and were never again to flourish, so that when the smaller combos took up behop, a gulf opened up between jazz and popular music that has not closed to this day. Rock 'n' roll was the foremost music that rushed to fill the gap. As behop persisted into the middle 1950's, the public looked back into the "race-music" repertoire to find a simple beat it could use for dancing.

The man probably most responsible for turning the Negro rhythm and blues into the all-American rock 'n' roll was disc jockey Alan Freed. In 1951, Freed was employed by a Cleveland radio station, where he became one of the first white DJ's to concentrate on rhythm and blues. He claims to have invented the term "rock 'n' roll." . . . In 1954, station WINS brought Freed to New York expressly to push rock 'n' roll. In 1955, Freed brought an interracial rock-'n'-roll vaudeville show into the Brooklyn Paramount for Easter and Labor Day weeks, and took a record gross

each time; during Labor Day week of 1956 he grossed
$221,000.

The first rock-'n'-roll record cut by a white artist
was probably Bill Haley's "Crazy Man Crazy," which
was recorded in 1951 and eventually sold a million
singles, but mostly on reissues from 1954 to 1956. Haley
came up with his first big money-maker, "Rock Around
the Clock," in 1953, but the rock-'n'-roll recording
boom did not begin until the summer of 1954, when
an unknown Negro group, the Chords, cut "Sh-Boom"
for a previously unknown label on the West Coast,
Cat. In a matter of weeks "Sh-Boom" was the Number
1 hit in Los Angeles. Then Mercury "covered" "Sh-
Boom" with a recording by an unknown group of
whites, the Crewcuts, and they had a national smash
record. For the next year and a half, as critic Arnold
Shaw points out, rhythm and blues had to be white-
washed before a given song could become a hit.

The recording supervisors for the larger labels could
not judge rhythm and blues; so rather than trust themselves to hire original rock-'n'-roll artists, they pre-
ferred at first to copy the hit records of smaller companies. An egregious example was "Tweedle-Dee-Dee,"
as recorded by LaVern Baker, whose arrangement was
lifted note for note by Georgia Gibbs. The McGuire
Sisters copied "Sincerely" from the Moonglows and
sold six times as many records. Dorothy Collins took
Clyde McPhatter's "Seven Days"; Perry Como took
"Kokomo" from Gene and Eunice; Teresa Brewer
took "A Tear Fell" from Ivory Joe Hunter; and Bill
Haley took Joe Turner's "Shake Rattle and Roll" and
sold 2,000,000 copies. Pat Boone, who has written a
book of moral and religious advice for teen-agers,

took "Ain't That a Shame?" from Fats Domino, "I'll Be Home" from the Flamingos, and "I Almost Lost My Mind" from Ivory Joe Hunter.

Then suddenly the tide began to turn, and imitators started to fail. Teresa Brewer failed to take "You Send Me" from Sam Cooke; Georgia Gibbs failed to take "Great Balls of Fire" from Jerry Lee Lewis; no one even tried to take "Blueberry Hill" from Fats Domino — and Cooke, Lewis, and Domino had themselves hits. Finally, a white southern boy named Elvis Presley — who has said that his greatest influences were the Negro blues singers Joe Turner and Big Bill Crudup — came up with a style all his own in "Heartbreak Hotel" and went on to become the biggest money-maker in the field without "covering" anyone.

Paralleling the rise of rock 'n' roll was what may prove to be the most significant technological development in the history of the mass media: the sudden spread of TV into nearly every home in the country. As of January, 1962, 90 per cent of the dwelling places in America had at least one TV set, and there were 60,000,000 sets in operation. The great service television performed for rock 'n' roll was to kill the big network radio shows and vacate the air space for local disc jockeys. Radio time had to be filled by popular music interspersed with commercials, and it was soon proven that the music that got the most calls and sold the most goods was rock 'n' roll.

Yet to describe rock 'n' roll in terms of its history is not completely to account for its unprecedented popularity, which has lasted now far past the point where mere fads peter out. Why, after ten years, does rock 'n' roll still get the most calls and sell the most goods?

The answer is that there is a general need for rock 'n' roll — a need rooted in strong feelings, a need fulfilled only by the one standard ingredient of all rock 'n' roll: its steady, heavy, simple beat.

When the listener submits himself to the beat, he loosens his mind from its moorings in space and time; no longer does he feel a separation between himself and his surroundings. The difficult world of external objects is blurred and unreal; only the inner pulse is real, the beat its outer projection. Earthly worries are submerged in a tide of rising exaltation. Dream and dreamer merge, object and feeling jell: the whole universe is compressed into the medium of the beat, where all things unite and pound forward, rhythmic, regular, not to be denied.

Rock 'n' roll is the only form in modern music which deliberately seeks these effects and no others. They are also obtainable through jazz, but the soul of jazz is its continual improvisation, which draws on a wide range of moods and which demands the keenest attention. In contrast, rock 'n' roll dulls the capacity for attention; the steady beat creates instead a kind of hypnotic monotony. Seen in this light, rock 'n' roll is only the latest in a series of rituals which have existed in many societies for the purpose of inducing mystic ecstasy, usually in connection with religion. One might think not only of African or American Indian drumbeating frenzies, but also of the cults of frenzied dancing and shaking which periodically rose up from the main body of European Christianity. In the United States, Negro "gospel music" often creates ecstasy

Pat Boone

through repeated phrases of enormous energy, and has been more than casually influential in the formation of rock 'n' roll. Through gospel music, rock 'n' roll draws directly on both Christian and African cults of rhythmic ecstasy. It should not surprise us then that so many rock-'n'-roll songs celebrate the all-pervasiveness of God.

But one should not take rock-'n'-roll lyrics too literally, for it is the rhythm of rock 'n' roll that carries its psychic message. "Positive" lyrics are mostly a sop to minds that do not want to know what they are thinking. In a record studio, I heard one of the most gifted rock-'n'-roll songwriters recording a trial version of a "pop-gospel" song. As he sang, I became increasingly aware that the subconscious thrust of the rhythm was completely undercutting the conscious intention of the lyrics. Pounding the piano with eyes shut in ecstatic pain, his voice cracking with raw emotion, the songwriter sang of a "He" who is always "in sight," even in the darkest night. But the music itself rocked on and out, away from the words and into a new wild night of nihilism where there is nothing yes nothing yes yes nothing no one but me and my sound and my rock. And why not? Believe in God — why not? In the darkest night it's all the same — words long gone. The message was false false false, yet it was true. The singer was groaning, growling, screaming, moaning, roaring — giving vent in the only way available to feelings genuinely his, regardless of the words he sang.

A secular approach only makes more obvious the sexual components of rhythmic ecstasy. The next song recorded by the songwriter was an urban rock, designed to express the feelings of a young man, living in a tenement. According to the lyrics, the main feature of tenement life is a certain "she" who is "waiting right there" and who "gives me everything." Taken literally, such lyrics are an outrageous lie; yet in the context of the music, one could feel them coming through with some truth. Of course tenements are not transformed into pleasure palaces by a magic she who can give everything, but one can try — one can give everything one's got. Even though the songwriter had never lived in a tenement, even though he was calculating probing the market with any lyrics he thought might appeal, and even though he was imitating Negro accents and phrasings not natural to him, he was communicating something real. I was moved. As I pounded the table in the listening booth, a clot of frustration thickened inside me and then purged itself. Or so I think. At any rate, I felt some momentary release.

Others, too, must find some emotional satisfaction in rock 'n' roll. For it has swept the world, achieving successes unknown to any previous popular music. In Britain, for example, riots broke out at each movie starring Presley or Haley. Queen Elizabeth herself requested a special screening of Haley's "Rock Around the Clock." And Haley in the flesh, a former hillbilly singer, was hired as star performer for the Duke of Kent's twenty-first birthday party. . . .

Though rock 'n' roll is broadcast all over our land and listened to by citizens of every description, most rock-'n'-roll records are bought by girls and boys between the ages of thirteen and fifteen. It seems, in fact, that every American in that age group collects 45 rpm singles. A rock-'n'-roll songwriter explained to me that

"at ages thirteen through fifteen, kids have a real community. At that time, everything they do is done together and done identically. Afterward, they spread
out, go separate ways, conform to a more complex
level." By the time the teen-ager is ready for greater
complexity, however, rock 'n' roll has already made a
permanent home for itself in his mental life. It has
played a definite part in preparing the teen-ager to
"spread out"; and even after he stops buying the
records, he will accept the sound of rock 'n' roll as
part of his everyday-noise background, just as city
dwellers accept the sounds of traffic. We might ask
ourselves, therefore, just why is it that with the onset
of puberty, Americans embrace rock 'n' roll? What
exactly does it do for them?

Whether he likes it or not, the adolescent is faced
with the problem of becoming an adult. He is no longer
a child, and his opportunities for play must be increasingly curtailed. Already he must start making the
choices which are intended to confine him to one education, one occupation, and one sexual partner. At any
rate, he must somehow join this society and live within its values. In giving up childhood, he gives up his
precious freedom and irresponsibility. It is inevitable
that the adolescent must feel intense frustration, and
also a need to express that frustration — to get it off
his chest. It is my contention that rock 'n' roll is
doubly helpful to the adolescent: it simultaneously
socializes him and provides a relatively harmless outlet for antisocial feeling. Does this seem a contradic-
tion? Well, why not? Just as many modern adults
pick themselves up with stimulants only to calm themselves with tranquilizers, so much of the surface stabil-

ity of our society is maintained by forces which, like rock 'n' roll, produce agitation only for the sake of quelling it. Like the teen-ager, each of us keeps moving all the time as a substitute for getting somewhere.

Rock 'n' roll is always doing two things at once. If it seems to be encouraging riot and destruction, note that it is dissipating riotous and destructive impulses before they can be turned into action. If its lyrics seem to purvey a "wholesome" message, the orgiastic thump of the beat will carry along with it the wildest fantasies. In short, through exposure to rock 'n' roll, teen-agers learn to handle their aggressions and discontents. . . .

There is still one more way in which rock 'n' roll helps bridge the gap between childhood and the threatening world of adult independence. To the 18,000,000 teen-agers who spend $10,000,000,000 every year in the consumer market, rock 'n' roll provides a special product by which to identify themselves. Others may listen to rock 'n' roll, but it belongs to the teen-ager. He pays for it; and when he hears it on the radio all day long, he can be satisfied that he has bought a place for himself in the world of consumption. For just as clothing manufacturers now tailor adult clothes along the lines originally developed "specially" for teen-age apparel, so adult America takes rock 'n' roll for its national music. With what care the teen-ager is eased into the satisfactions of consumption as a way of life! First, special products all his own to practice on — music, clothes, magazines, movies; then the gradual absorption of these products by the adult culture, so that as the teen-ager grows older, he will never have to make an abrupt break with the products he knows how to use. . . .

ONE NEAR SQUARE WHO DOESN'T KNOCK THE ROCK

James Michener

Not quite a square, but by no means a hipster either, famed novelist James Michener found himself propelled into a fascinating world when called upon to be a judge at a recent rock-'n'-roll world championship. What were his impressions? First, that the young contestants were above average in looks, cleanliness, charm, and good manners. Second, that their musical instruments were less important than the electronic systems that reproduce them and throw them full volume at the listener. Indeed, the cacaphony of sound produced by these systems when the bands were tuning up made the most lasting impression. Third, that he came away rather liking rock 'n' roll — not as a steady diet perhaps, but the way he likes pepper in cooking, as a vital accent.

When my neighbor, St. John Terrell, proprietor of the Music Circus, a theater in a tent in Lambertville, New Jersey, advised me that he had picked me to be one of the judges in the finals of his nationwide rock-'n'-roll world championship, I thought he must be out of his cotton-pickin' mind.

"Imagine!" he cried persuasively. "You'll be sitting there with Cousin Brucey on one side and Phil Spector on the other, and you'll be deciding the fate of American music."

"Who is Cousin Brucey?" I asked.

Terrell gasped. "You mean you're not with it? You mean you don't listen to one of the most significant forces in the power structure today? You mean . . ."

"O.K. So who's Phil Spector?"

The look this time was compassionate, and from his pocket Terrell produced a newspaper article which showed an extraordinary young man in his early twenties, with very long hair, dressed in exquisite clothes, and possessed of one of the sharpest physiognomies I have seen in many years. The article informed teenagers that their purchase of the records he produces had made him a millionaire three times over.

The fourth judge was to be Harry Haenigsen, the cartoonist, a dignified square who would wear normal clothes and with whom I would at least be able to talk while Cousin Brucey and Phil Spector were communicating with the teen-agers. I agreed, and in doing so propelled myself into a fascinating world.

To my astonishment, more than 400 bands from all parts of America had applied for entry blanks and eighty-eight had been chosen to report to the big tent in Lambertville for the initial weeding out. (The finals would be held on Labor Day.) The winning band would receive $1,000 in cash, a television appearance, a chance to cut a record, and a hopeful start on the road to a professional career. When I awakened to the excitement this contest had generated, I decided to take some time off to talk with the contestants and to discover what was happening in their world.

I began with the average adult's sketchy information about rock 'n' roll. I had spent an apprenticeship at the Dom, the Greenwich Village headquarters of this cult, watching with envy as youngsters did the Watusi and the Frug I had checked in at Arthur, which had one of the best groups of musicians on hand I'd heard in a long time. And throughout most of the countries of Europe I had found rock the prevailing choice of teen-agers.

I had also watched on television such shows as "Hullabaloo" and "Shindig." I knew the Beatles and Elvis and the Dave Clark Five. I thought "Downtown" one of the most compelling songs of this decade and had even spent my own money to buy a copy of the record because I felt it to be a next step in the classic tradition of "One O'Clock Jump" and "The Saints Go Marching In."

I wasn't entirely a square, but I wasn't hip, either. When the new sound was well played, I liked it. And as a novelist, I was fascinated by the sociology that accompanied the mania: the long hair, the Edwardian elegance among boys who would normally be repelled by such fashion, the cabalistic jargon, the tempting experiment with marijuana and LSD, the phenomenon of teen-age screaming, and, most important of all, the presence of great protest.

I began my job of judging by reading the stack of applications, and quickly learned that to these young men music was certainly more important than spelling: the Vandles of Northumberland (Pennsylvania), the Infinits of Brooklyn, the Tormenters of Virginia. The Limitations, also from Brooklyn, announced that they were going to play "Hi Heal Sneakers."

But along with the near illiteracy came the voice of great aspiration, and no one could read these letters without feeling a sense of identification with the writers. Said the Telestars of Trenton, "We are all eager to get ahead and make something of ourselves." One letter exemplified almost ideally the basic attitudes of these bands: "The accordion player is studying music he looks forward to a brake in show business he can play any thing. Our sax man is tops with great showman ship his playing has made many a young fellow envey him. This is a fine good all american team i as there manager enjoy helping them when ever i can."

It was a blazing hot summer afternoon when I reported for the first of the elimination contests, and as the bands arrived and began to unpack their gear I received my first shock. I had expected groups of four or five musicians, carrying guitars, perhaps a double bass and a set of drums. Little Caesar and His Romans from Lewiston, Maine, disabused me. The five young men arrived in a private car, followed by a truck from which they took a dozen large electronic speakers, five amplifiers, four additional microphones, an organ requiring four men to carry it, and literally hundreds of feet of special electric cord.

I asked Ronald Poulin, the sixteen-year-old leader of the group, how much money his boys had invested in their equipment, and he suggested the following, although he didn't have accurate figures at hand:

One organ	$1,500
Complete set of drums	750
Two saxophones	400
Two guitars	1,600
Amplifiers, mikes, etc.	525
Music for 120 songs	100
Trailer	800

All this equipment had been paid for by the money these five boys, the oldest eighteen, had earned playing in night clubs, at birthday parties, and at the Friday-night Pal Hops held by the city of Lewiston, at which 1,500 kids regularly appear.

All members of Poulin's team spoke French, took music lessons, and could play four or five different instruments. At the end of my questions, Poulin volunteered, "One of the best things about our group is that not one boy has ever been in trouble." (I thought, "Earning the money you have tied up in your gear would keep you too busy.") Poulin added, "We all expect to graduate from high school."

The cost figure for the Little Caesars was by no means the highest, because these boys had no reverberator chambers, no echo boxes, no pillow speakers, and no special amplifiers for their organ. In questioning other groups, I found that $2,000 was about the minimum and $6,000 not unusual. I also learned that in many cases parents, enticed by the money earned by the Beatles, had supplied both the initial cash and the impetus. It was not unusual to read on an application blank: "Leader Mike Provenzio age 17. Manager Lila Provenzio age 37." During the entire World Championship the judges ran into only one bit of unpleasantness, when a distracted mother threatened to tear the tent apart if her son's band was not given a higher rating. "I could tell they were the best by just listening," she said.

From helping the bands unpack I gained two distinct impressions which never left me. First, the young men engaged in this wild and passionate art form are above average in looks, cleanliness, charm, and good manners.

Even those who featured outlandish garb (the Prophets of Fredericksburg, Virginia, appeared in togas and leather shoes whose thongs criss-crossed to their knees, while the Monkey Men of Yardville, New Jersey, played from inside a cage which they carried with them) were orderly and delightful to be with.

Second, the musical instrument of itself seems to be less important than the electronic systems that reproduce it and throw it full volume at the listener. If — and this happened during the finals — the electricity happens to go off, the music of this generation subsides into a meaningless whisper. Five amplifiers and four mikes were about the least a self-respecting band could get away with.

One aspect of the rock-'n'-roll world took me by surprise. Each of the bands carried a supply of formal calling cards. (Favored were highly marbelized ones in pastel 1890 colors with rounded corners and florid printing styles.) These cards are presented to new groups when introductions are made; and if one watches bands assembling, it is like observing a convention of bullfighters or actors or other professionals. A stately formalism prevails.

I was also surprised by the lack of Negro musicians. If the 400 bands whose histories I studied were typical, rock 'n' roll is largely a white phenomenon. Could it be that the cost of the required electrical gear excludes the Negro? Was it an accident that the two bands with the most complete electronic gear carried off the $1,000 and $500 prizes?

On the first day I attended, forty-three bands were competing. They were arranged side by side in an enormous circle around the outer edge of the circus tent, while the judges sat at desks on the stage in the center, turning to face each of the contestants as they began. I wish everyone who wanted an introduction to rock 'n' roll could have been there in those five minutes before the trials started. Some 200 musicians, each with his amplifier turned on full volume, ran through his private problems for the last time. It was noise such as the world has rarely heard — absolute cacophony, metallic, brash, the sound of our age.

I don't know for how long the human ear could stand such noise as we heard that day, but I must confess I rather liked it. It hurtled at me from all sides, from some 400 amplifiers, and was as near to total noise as anything I have so far experienced. A music manufacturer had approached Mr. Terrell some days earlier, proposing that he be allowed to supply all contestants with the instruments to be used in the finals. His argument was: "I don't make the best musical instruments in the country, but I do make the loudest. Our engineers have come up with a new electronic circuit which eliminates all the old-style music and produces instead the perfect metallic sound."

He demonstrated the new development with one of his guitars. Today's guitar is solid wood; the old-fashioned vibrating chamber had to be eliminated because it produces music with unwanted overtones rather than an uncontaminated metallic impulse which can be amplified electronically. I recognized the sound coming out of this manufacturer's new-style guitar as the one that I had grown to like in "hard" rock-'n'-roll

Nat "King" Cole

bands, and during the ensuing contests I invariably found myself voting for the band that could produce precisely this sound.

In the songs of rock 'n' roll, if indeed they can be called songs, I noticed the advent of much protest music stemming in a direct line from ballads like Nat King Cole's success of 1951, "They Tried to Tell Us We're Too Young." In one song the leader of the pack is killed in a motorcycle crash, but that is all right because he died living up to the code of his gang. In another, the musicians lament the fate of the world: If they cleaned things up in Viet Nam, there'd still be Selma, Alabama. One song which gained enthusiastic approval told of how a boy was refused admission to high school because his hair was too long. Terrell explained, "Rock is being married to folk music, and the offspring is protest."

On the day of the finals I met for the first time Cousin Brucey, a tall, handsome, well-groomed, and literate young man. His radio and television schedules (he is a disc jockey for ABC) had necessitated arriving by helicopter, and he asked if I would excuse him while he slipped into an iridescent blue and silver suit that was notably more dignified — even reserved — than it sounds. He had an extraordinary way with the teen-agers who crowded the tent and referred constantly to his radio and television shows, which apparently have an enormous impact on younger people along the Eastern Seaboard.

"It may surprise you," he told me, "to know that my most important following is in the colleges. They don't have too much time to listen to music, and they know they can trust me to spot the new trends."

Along the edge of the crowd I noticed an important political leader, a man with an advanced degree in music, whom one would not expect to be interested in rock. "I'm not," he said, "but my kids heard that Cousin Brucey was going to be here and they consider him more significant than Albert Schweitzer, Adlai Stevenson, and John F. Kennedy together."

We had received some evidence of the disc jockey's power sometime earlier. Mr. Terrell had risked his shirt by importing the Righteous Brothers, in hopes they would fill his tent at two and three dollars a head; but ticket sales were deplorable, and the affair was about to be a bust when an expert on such matters asked, "Have you advertised?"

Terrell said that he always did, and the man asked, "Where?" Terrell rattled off the names of the newspapers, and the man expressed amazement. "Newspapers? The people who come to hear the Righteous Brothers never read. Get on the radio. That's all they listen to."

So Terrell called a disc jockey, who made a brief comment on his show to the effect that all the cousins who were really in the know were trekking on down to the Music Circus to hear the living greatest. And within a few hours all seats were sold.

At one point in Bruce's dialogue with his fans a young man asked, "Cousin Brucey, it says here that points will be awarded for showmanship. What's showmanship?" Cousin Brucey thought for a moment, made two false starts, then pointed to an astonishing young man approaching the stage and cried, "Here's showmanship."

It was Phil Spector, the twenty-four-year-old king of the rocks. He wore a skin-tight Edwardian suit with the

narrowest trousers I've yet seen. (Explained one contestant when I asked about trousers, "You might say,
Mr. Michener, that any boy in this competition would
rather drop dead than put his pants on after he had put
his shoes on." Another boy said, "Frankly, if you can
pull your trousers on over your shoes, neither the
trousers nor the shoes are worth wearing.")

Spector also wore a jazzy white-lace cavalier shirt
with the biggest ruffles at the cuffs so far made, plus
sharply pointed boots with three-inch heels. His hair
was beyond my powers of description: a kind of real
wig hanging down to his shoulders and teased into a
wonderful bundle. The kids in the audience went wild
with approval.

In the judging arena, Spector told me, "You listen
for the lead voice. If he can convey, the band can make
it."

"What else do you listen for?"

"A total beat. If they have a total beat, they can make
it."

It quickly became apparent that the World Championship would go either to the long-haired, very clever
Rockin' Paramounts of Buffalo, New York, or to the
controlled, big-tone Galaxies of Trenton, New Jersey.
The Paramounts were handicapped by the fact that two
of their band had to be lifted onto the stage before they
could play. One was sick with mononucleosis and had
covered the distance from Buffalo in an improvised
ambulance; another, with long flowing hair, had
broken something while playing football. But when
they were propped up they played like demons, and I
shudder to think what they might have accomplished in

good health. Cousin Brucey whispered, "These boys are bound to become top professionals."

The Galaxies featured the hardest, most metallic sound heard in the competition, plus a wild rhythm and a screaming vocal. They had perfected a clever way of ending each number with a coda in which tempo, key, frenzy, and volume were all accelerated (I shouted to Haenigsen, "At last I know what escalation means"), so they had to be declared the winners.

It was a popular verdict. Each of the last six bands was of professional quality. As soon as the winners had been announced, things started happening. The Merv Griffin television show. An invitation to cut a record. Engagements in areas unexplored before. And that good old $1,000 in cash to pay for some fresh electronic equipment.

My lasting impressions of the World Championship are varied. I found that I liked rock-'n'-roll music the way I like pepper in cooking: not as a steady diet, but appreciated as a vital accent. I especially like the young people who made the music, my favorite contestant being sixteen-year-old Jon Van Eaton, leader of the Trees from Trenton. Jon has studied music, plays the guitar, clarinet, bass, sax, oboe, bassoon, harmonica, English horn, and flute. He says of his group, "We try to be gentlemen and scholars, and I suppose I'll go on to college. If I make it, it'll be because music paid the way."

The best thing about the competition was that incredible five minutes when the bands were tuning up (tuning their electronics, that is, not their instruments). But the experience I shall not soon forget was a report on the Impostors of New York, written by their fourteen-year-old drummer. This letter seems to me to summarize what rock 'n' roll means to many teen-agers:

> Our group is one which can make good and go professional. Even though we are only fifteen we have the most natural music talent in Peter Cooper Village or Stuyvesant Town either. Our leader, Barry Flast, is a very outstanding person. He writes music like there is no tomorrow. Already he has written 50 songs. He like myself feels a strange new power when we play. All of us love our music; to us it is the second most important thing except school. When I get up on that stage to practice I feel as if I could cry because nobody is around to hear us. Our parents say give up: stop dreaming. But I listen to the radio and say to myself: Oh if only Cousin Brucey could hear the songs played by we Impostors. Would they sound professional to him? I say they would if we touched them up a bit.
>
> Very truly yours,
MARK LITT

P.S. Barry Flast has said my feel for the drums is remarkable. He says I am an empressionist as well as a great drummer; that is one of the reasons this group is on the ball.

The reason why the Impostors couldn't get to the World Championship was a crisis common to such groups: their families had taken them to five different locales for their vacations, and they couldn't get together for practice.

About the Authors

BRUCE JAY FRIEDMAN is the author of two novels, *Stern* and *A Mother's Kisses*, and a book of short stories, *Far from the City of Class*. He has also contributed articles and stories to *Esquire*, *The Saturday Evening Post*, and *The New Yorker*, among others. Born April 26, 1930, he earned a Bachelor of Journalism degree from the University of Missouri in 1951. Mr. Friedman is married and the father of three children.

PETER BART picked up the California sound while serving as a West Coast correspondent for *The New York Times*, a position he has held since 1960. Besides the *Atlantic Monthly*, Mr. Bart has contributed to *Harper's*, *Esquire*, and *The Saturday Review*. Mr. Bart was born in New York City July 24, 1932. He obtained a B.A. from Swarthmore in 1954 and later attended the London School of Economics for one year. He is married and has two children.

LOUIE ROBINSON is West Coast editor of *Ebony* magazine, with which he has been associated since 1953. Recently he completed a juvenile book on tennis player Arthur Ashe, which he expects to be published soon. Born in Dallas, Texas, October 4, 1926, he attended Lincoln University at Jefferson City, Missouri. Mr. Robinson is married to the former Mati Hucaby.

ALFRED G. ARONOWITZ recently went from writing about rock-'n'-roll groups to managing them, including one called The Myddle Class. In his spare time he is also working on several books. A former newspaperman and contributor to *The Saturday Evening Post*, Mr. Aronowitz is the author of *Ernest Hemingway: the Life and Death of a Man*. He was born May 20, 1928 in Bordentown, New Jersey, and obtained a Bachelor of Letters degree from Rutgers in 1950. He is married and the father of three children.

VERNON SCOTT has been chronicling the lives of movie and TV stars since 1953, when he became Hollywood correspondent of the United Press. He is also a busy free-lance, contributing to, among others, *The Saturday Evening Post*, *The Ladies' Home Journal*, and *Cosmopolitan* magazines. Mr. Scott was born in San Francisco February 13, 1923. He attended Ohio State University before graduating from the University of Southern California in 1949. A family man, Mr. Scott is married and has two children.

HENRIETTA YURCHENCO is one of the world's leading authorities on folk music. She began her career in 1939 with the inception of her WNYC, New York, radio program, "Adventures in Folk Music." Since then she has traveled widely to record examples of the art. Besides conducting her radio program, she teaches courses in Folk Music of the World at the New School for Social Research and City College in New York, and is currently at work on a book. She is married to an architect, Irving Levine, and has a grown son who plays Indian music.

TOM WOLFE, no relation to his famous namesake, was born
and grew up in Richmond, Virginia. He was graduated from
Washington and Lee University and took his doctorate at
Yale. Mr Wolfe has been with the *New York Herald Tribune*
since 1962, writing regularly for the paper's Sunday
magazine, *New York*, as well as for *Esquire* and *Harper's
Bazaar*. His article, "The First Tycoon of Teen," appears in
a collection of his essays entitled, *The Kandy-Colored
Tangerine-Flake Streamline Baby*.

JEREMY LARNER won two awards in 1964, the Delta Prize
for his novel, *Drive, He Said,* and the Aga Khan Prize from
The Paris Review for the best short story of that year. He is
also co-author of a book of interviews with heroin addicts,
The Addict in the Street, as well as a contributor to numerous
magazines. Mr. Larner was born March 20, 1937, and
received a B.A. from Brandeis University in 1958.

JAMES A. MICHENER is the author of many books, including
Tales of the South Pacific, for which he won a Pulitzer Prize
in 1948, *The Bridges at Toko-Ri, Sayonara, Hawaii,* and
most recently, *The Source.* Rodgers and Hammerstein made
his *Tales of the South Pacific* into a memorable Broadway
musical which, like others of his works, was later brought
to the screen. Mr. Michener is a *summa cum laude* from
Swarthmore College, 1929. Born in New York City February
3, 1907, Mr. Michener is married to Mari Yoriko Sabusawa.

YEAH
YEAH
YEAH